Life Sentence
Life Purpose

Mickey Owens and Kim Whiting
© amazon.com 2012

Editorial Consultants:
K. Large and Carter Blackwell

Media, business and other inquiries, contact:
Kim Whiting
whitingk@cox.net
(702) 524-3231

"The degree of civilization in a society can best be judged by entering its prisons."- Dostoevsky

Dedicated to Uncle Gordon, for being there for me all these years and typing in the original pages of the manuscript—Mickey

Note

Many of the stories in this memoir were sent to me piecemeal in Mickey's letters. Some were not even intended for the book, but simply stories Mickey wanted to share with me. I did my best to put them in the correct sequence/correct institution, but even so, Mickey has told me that I'm "slightly off" in my sequencing of a couple of the California institutions. While the sequencing of this book may be "slightly off" in one section, the stories are just as real and accurate as Mickey can recall them. I'm sure you'll find that the order they're in or the institution they're attributed to doesn't diminish their power.

Some names have been changed to protect privacy.

Introduction

Mickey lives in Pleasant Valley State Prison; which is one of the best misnomers I've ever heard. It wasn't considerate of me, but I burst out laughing when I looked at the prison on Google Satellite. I thought of the guys who found a small continent covered in ice and called it "Greenland." They must have chuckled all the way home. What I'd like to do is let the inmates of PVSP send submissions for what *they* think their home should be called. Much of it wouldn't be printable, but I'm sure they (and I) would get a kick out of that. In defense of whoever named the place Pleasant Valley, it appears they got it half right. It does look like a valley and it has mountains on one side, but it's no Shenandoah. Even a desert-lover like me wouldn't find it pleasant.

Mickey and I were brought together by what felt like design. I was collecting inspirational short stories from prison inmates, with the hope of making them into a book. A woman at a prison outreach organization in California said she didn't have any stories, but she had just read an inmate's manuscript and thought he was a talented writer. She thought he might have some inspirational stories to tell and gave me his California address. I wrote him asking for uplifting short stories regarding his prison life. Instead of sending short stories, he sent an entire manuscript. A manuscript was not what I wanted to read. A manuscript was not going to help me get my collection of inspirational stories done. I moaned—I sighed --and then read it anyway.

By page two, I learned that Mickey is from Oklahoma, which after moving twenty-seven times, happens to be where I now live. I instantly bonded with Mickey's story and knew I was going to be a part of it. Before I was even halfway through reading it, I offered to help Mickey complete and publish it.

While working with Mickey on this book, I have experienced a stream of serendipity—the kind that gives me goose bumps. For example, I discovered that Mickey had lived a mile away from me in Las Vegas during his short stint as a free man. He spent homeless nights in the same dry streambed that I ran down almost every morning. I often said "hello" to the homeless guys I encountered and Mickey may very well have been one of them. I could take this as just another small world experience, but I think it's more a demonstration of the way in which souls travel in ever tighter circles as they get ready to cross paths.

There's been a strong sense of the familiar surrounding our collaboration, as if we've done this before or all along. Mickey felt it immediately too and in one of his earliest letters said, "You and I have known each other a very long time and it's nice to finally meet." In that seemingly nonsensical statement, he perfectly described what I have been feeling. He nailed it.

But let me say that this process has not been all harmony and goose bumps. It has been an exercise in trust for Mickey and me –trust in each other as well as in the Power that seems to be orchestrating this process. Our faith in both has been challenged at times. There have been days when my gut has felt like churning tar, but this tar has paved the way for some personal healing. I know that Mickey has also healed through the telling of his story and the collaboration.

Mickey entered his first home designed for "corrections" at the age of eleven and I'd guess that he's lived in about eight more since then. He's a "lifer" in every sense of the word. His current home is where the most violent and hardened criminals reside. Most live there for the remainder of their lives. It's the kind of facility that has steel doors on the cells instead of bars, the kind of place so filled with human misery and rage that it's often on security "lockdown," meaning that the inmates aren't allowed out of their cells at all, often for days on end.

Most of the men in this prison meet the "three strikes and you're out" requirement, or more accurately, "three strikes and you're in." "Three strikes" refers to having committed at least three felonies, two of them violent. Mickey has had his three strikes. In fact, sandwiched between his several felonies is murder. Mickey has killed a man. By the time I discovered this fact, I had received a handful of letters from Mickey. It was difficult to reconcile the person he was in his letters with the person who had committed murder.

In his letters, Mickey comes across as someone always on the lookout for beauty or a bright side to the situation. He talks a lot about how he sees and feels Spirit moving in his life. He seems quiet and bookish – uses large words –and leans toward the philosophical. I don't know whether Mickey is gifted with an exceptional memory or if he simply reads the same books year after year, but he can --and does-- quote everything from the Bible to Course in Miracles to Taoist wisdom. His memory is not as keen when it comes to the emotional details of his life, but that's understandable. If I had lived Mickey's life, I too would've spent most of my fifty-six years working on forgetting. Mickey comes across as extremely sensitive and vulnerable —someone deeply affected by the lack of light, beauty, kindness and connection in his environment. He is prone to slipping into darkness and fearfulness if he's not constantly vigilant of his thoughts and outlook. Mickey has had to work doubly hard to overcome his fearfulness, a fearfulness that has at times crossed into paranoia. I once asked him to complete the sentence "Life is unfair because..." and he wrote "because I have always felt afraid."

There is very little light or beauty in a maximum security prison and there is also little beauty through the small windows —and when I describe them as "small," I mean small. The windows are no more than three inches across. Mickey says a man couldn't stick his arm through them. What beauty once lived outside the walls in Pleasant Valley was killed by herbicides, because prison officials don't want to give escapees a place to hide.

The closest the men come to "communing with nature" is two to four hours on specified days, in a prison yard with about a thousand other incarcerated men. Jobs are scarce and the men spend years on a waiting list to get janitorial and other grunt jobs. There's very little to do and even fewer ways to make a contribution and feel of value. Mickey says that the idleness of the time spent there is what most makes it feel like "doing time."

When love shows up at all at Pleasant Valley, it's in small doses. The prison is in a remote location and many of the inmates have family far way. Mickey hasn't had a single visitor in eight years.

To the unknowing observer, it would seem that God did not live where Mickey lives. In fact, it took Mickey years to realize that God can be found in a maximum security prison. He still loses sight of that sometimes.

In the free world, people heal and become better people through beauty, nature, being useful, love, support and connection with Spirit. A maximum security prison offers little if any opportunity for these. But there is an advantage to being disadvantaged, a silver lining in having little to nothing outside ourselves worth living for. Mickey is not distracted by the external assistance of things like beauty and love. He has discovered that the only place left to go is within-- and that within is buried treasure. Mickey said it nicely in a letter: *"Not much time is spent dwelling on the past or future. The past holds regrets and memories that our lives will never repeat. The future is just more of the same. Most of us here will die here and it's not a thought anyone cares to entertain. But this letting go can help you. It is in the now that the Divine can bless us. In this way, we are much like trappist monks, exchanging external comforts for what is within. As the Bible says, 'For where your treasure is, there will your heart be also.'"*

Mickey lives a monk-like existence. Like the subgroups of almost all major religions who sequester themselves from the world, Mickey spends much of his time in meditation, quiet contemplation and acts of kindness. But his life has not always been this quiet. "Tumultuous" is too gentle a word to describe his youthful years. "Disastrous" is probably a better word. Mickey may have the worst timing of anyone I've ever met. He (a white Okie) entered an almost all-black correctional school right after Martin Luther King was assassinated. He entered prison for the first time just a couple days before one of the biggest and most violent prison riots in history. Most of his subsequent prisons have also decided to hold riots shortly after his arrival.

Mickey may be the person they had in mind when the phrase, "He fell through the cracks" was coined. But then, Mickey was born in 1955 when the cracks were large. Over time, those cracks have been filled with such things as head start programs, youth and family counseling, specialized education, kinder and more effective reward-consequence strategies, mentorship programs for children of the incarcerated, more effective addiction counseling, in-house prison outreach programs and re-entry programs upon release from prison. But Mickey came into life before that. He's had to jump life's hurdles without that extra assistance and has not been the most agile jumper.

But he's had his writing. The man can write. According to Mickey, writing has always been the one consistent bright spot for him. His poetry and letters not only help him pass the time, but have been a safe emotional outlet for him when no other outlets were available. His writing has been both his therapy and his play –

and perhaps a large part of his purpose. He was born to write. More specifically, he was born to write this book.

When I received a photo of Mickey —the one featured on the back of this book —I sobbed and continued to burst into tears on and off for the rest of the evening. In his photo, Mickey looks like the sensitive, kind, clear soul that is conveyed in his letters. His eyes are sad, but peaceful, and his posture is gentle. It's ironic, but the descriptor that most readily comes to mind when looking at the photo – at a man who has spent almost forty years in correctional institutions and committed violent crimes, including murder is: Innocent.

The top photo is of a unit similar to Mickey's and the cell below is an almost exact match to Mickey's description of his cell, except that his window is about half as wide.

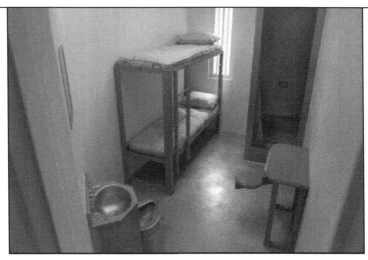

Pleasant Valley State Prison

Dad

"Do not search for the truth,
Only cease to cherish opinions."
3rd Zen Patriarch

It was 1972 and my father and I had been re-united after his latest stint in prison. I'd had very little contact with him during my upbringing because he had been in prison for most of it and mom divorced him as soon as he entered prison for the first time. But I think my dad was attracted to my mom even all those years later —just something I observed when he finally came around again. I understood. She was beautiful.

Dad had strawberry blonde hair that belied his Irish heritage. He and I were built about the same; slim in build and about 5' 7". I noticed that women were attracted to him. Both my parents got a lot of attention from the opposite sex. Dad was manipulative and controlling with me and even as a teen I could see through his manipulations, but I wanted to please him and build a relationship with him, so for the most part, I did his bidding.

He rented a small house in Oklahoma City in order to be near me and at his suggestion we hit the road together and traveled to Texas, simply for the sake of going somewhere together. I could tell he was doing his best to form some sort of relationship with me, but having been in prison most of his adult life, he had trouble with emotional openness —or maybe that was simply his personality. He was also very addicted to drugs —we both were —and our preoccupation with getting our next fix got in the way of true emotional connection.

A few days after we returned from our road trip, he suggested that we rob a few pharmacies. Because I was still sixteen, he figured the authorities would go easy on me if I were to get caught. He figured wrong. I already had an impressive rap sheet by that age and had only recently been released from eleven months of drug rehab. There wasn't a judge or legal authority alive who would think to go easy on me. One glance at my records and anyone could see that I was trouble with a capital "T."

During the eleven months of drug rehab, I had attended group therapy and gotten extensive individual counseling. Considering that this was the early 1970s, the program was a good one. But I don't know if there was a program in existence that would've been strong enough to get me to want to face life chemical-free. My life was already a string of pain and self-created failures. I was a loser from a long line of losers. I knew the kind of life that was possible for a guy like me and most certainly didn't want to go through it sober. If I couldn't lift myself any higher, then I would endure my low state from a chemically induced high.

On our third pharmacy robbery, I entered carrying a deceivingly real looking toy pistol (my dad and I had put black shoe polish on it to make it look more real) and read a list of the drugs that I wanted the pharmacist to hand me. My dad waited in the get-away car. We drove away without incident and I went to my mother's house, bringing along some of the drugs for her. The police traced the car to where he lived. When interrogated, he told them that I was the one who committed the crime and gave them directions to my mother's house. They arrested me and released him from custody because he had cooperated with them. I pled guilty and received a twenty-five-year prison sentence. He was killed in a car accident three years later. He didn't get the chance to say he was sorry, but I loved and missed him anyway. Now that I understand the forces of greed, self-loathing and desperation that come with drug addiction, I love him even more.

Crime Does Not Pay

It was a hot, dusty day; the only kind of day to be found in southern Oklahoma in late June. It was 1973 and the summer that would change my life and my world forever.

I had just turned eighteen. One year prior, I had been arrested for armed robbery. I didn't have the money for bail and my parents were too addicted to drugs to give up drug money, so I spent the trial and pre-sentencing in jail. Happily, jail wasn't the violent place that I had imagined, but the idleness and complete lack of novelty in any given day made my time there challenging. Playing poker with my cellmates was the only lasting diversion. We weren't allowed money, but several smuggled it in. I had pled guilty in court and after a year was sentenced to twenty-five years in the Oklahoma prison system.

Although I readily admitted my guilt, I did not feel much remorse for what I had done. I thought twenty-five years was excessive; I had, after all, used a toy pistol and not a real gun.

I was taken to the prison in the sheriff's car with a couple other new inmates. We were shackled with leg irons and handcuffs and I was extremely nervous about the older cons that I would soon be sharing time with. I had heard that rape and brutality were common in this prison and I wanted out before I even arrived. At the same time, echoes of Alcatraz, the Bastille, and a host of Hollywood-generated notions about incarceration filled my mind. I felt the thrill of adrenaline. I was, after all, a teenager.

As the Sheriff's car pulled to a stop in front of the Oklahoma State Penitentiary (OSP), with its high, white-washed walls, gun towers, and endless stream of bars, my curiosity became pure fear. The reality hit that this was to be my new residence for a very, very long time. I did not feel ready for this place-- but then, is a person ever ready for prison? The other two unfortunates in the car with me seemed as distressed and nervous as I felt. We had remained quiet throughout the journey, while the two cops in front had chatted amiably among themselves, as if they were out for a Sunday afternoon drive in the country. But then, we *were* driving through the countryside, so I suppose this was the case for them. Just another day at work.

After the removal of our chains we were escorted into a small, low building where we were stripped, deloused and showered. Our street clothing was taken and we were issued blue coveralls, mine a couple of sizes too large. I rolled up the long cuffs and figured it adequate.

A new guard arrived and escorted us through two locked gates, up a flight of stairs and into the main administration building. We traveled down a corridor, passing offices on both sides.

We reached the final barred gate that led into the prison rotunda and I noticed a sign posted above the doorway: "Crime Does Not Pay." A little late for that piece of wisdom, I thought.

Prisons are cold and indifferent places. They reflect the dark side of public opinion. But there are myths that Hollywood and the news media seek to exploit through sensationalism. Many in prison are not mean and callous, void of any sense of caring and compassion. Most are deserving of forgiveness. I suppose Jesus would say that we all are. I do not condone criminal behavior nor do I aspire to it. Many thousands in these prisons feel the same. We have made bad decisions and we are forced to face the consequences. We probably judge ourselves more intensely than those in the free world. Most of us are not the animals that those who know nothing of the circumstances that culminated in our arrival here think we are.

But I am not writing this book in an attempt to justify my behavior. It's up to the reader to make his or her own judgments. I am simply relating the experiences I have had in the hope that what I say might help you to better understand me and those like me --and our purpose in the scheme of things. I write with the hope that I too will better understand.

It is said that prisons do not rehabilitate prisoners, but teaches them how to be better criminals. When the Sheriff's car first brought me to the high walls of the Oklahoma prison, I was looking at spending twenty-five years there —an incomprehensible amount of time for an eighteen-year-old. It is now almost exactly forty years since I passed through those prison gates and I still call prison home. It is likely that I will spend the rest of my life here. Perhaps what they say about prison is true.

The Young and the Restless
This mug shot was taken when I entered the Oklahoma State Penitentiary. The date shown in the photo is June 18th, 1973. My eighteenth birthday had been on June 3rd. I remember trying to look tough for the photo, but I was more scared than I had ever been.

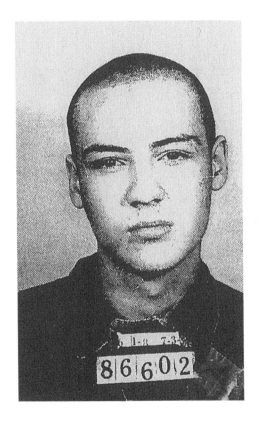

As "new fish," we were escorted to a "Receiving Cell," where we awaited classification into the system. The cell had two bunks, but was only five feet wide by eight feet deep. With its small size and hard surfaces, it looked and sounded like someone had created a bedroom out of a standard sized bathroom. But then, I suppose this was partly the case, since this small room also served as our bathroom. My cellmate and I would be sharing every bodily function in this tiny room. I could stand in the middle and touch both walls with my outstretched hands. The space, like almost every cell, was so tight that one man had to be on the bunk for the other to maneuver through. There was not enough room to pass one another. I felt totally crushed and claustrophobic. But in time I would adapt to small spaces.

One of the guys in the car with me on the way to the prison was named David. We became friends and because he had done time at this prison before, he was able to tell me how it was and what to expect. But the only time we were allowed out of our cells was at chow time, so we rarely got the chance to talk.

The energy of the new inmates was very tense, as if we were all in an airplane waiting for it to crash. I was sad about the life that loomed before me, but at eighteen, I wasn't able to comprehend twenty-five years of these circumstances.

I learned that the part of the brain responsible for comprehending the long-range future, including the long-term consequences of our actions, is not fully developed until the age of twenty-one. When I read this, I thought about kids who join the military at nineteen with brains not fully equipped to grasp what they are signing up for. I thought about me at sixteen, not fully able to comprehend the long-term ramifications of committing robbery. But entering prison at eighteen, this lack of long-range thinking was a blessing. I wasn't able to wrap my brain around the fact that I would be incarcerated for more years than I had been alive. I wasn't able to picture it. This was good, because simply focusing on being incarcerated at that moment was bleak enough.

I was grateful not to feel the menace or threat from the other inmates that I had expected. Those around me tended to ignore me. I later discovered that everyone has their own agenda in prison and a person is mostly ignored, unless he makes some kind of waves.

The guards were another matter. My first night in the Receiving cell, I was awakened by a hissing sound. A guard was spraying mace in my cell as he walked by on his rounds. I later learned that this was a form of initiation —a welcoming warning from my keepers. I choked and sneezed the remainder of the night, and morning brought red eyes and a seed of hostility that would germinate and grow. I understood that, ironically, injustice was part of the criminal justice system. It was part of prison life and I learned that it was easier to accept the inevitable than struggle with it.

The next thirty days on receiving cell passed in idleness. Being young, fresh, and new, many of the older convicts were giving me 'the look', which was an open invitation for sexual activity. I had been through it in county jail and knew what it meant. I ignored it. Homosexuality was rarely forced on anyone. The "look" was exactly that, it was a quiet invitation and it was the young man's decision whether to take the offer or not.

In those days, before AIDS, homosexuality was rampant in prison. Many young boys chose to be in relationship with an established inmate, whether out of a desire for a protector, or to feel special, or simply to have someone who cared about them, some semblance of family or relationship. It was a choice based on necessity: physical, emotional or mental. As much as I craved human contact and some approximation of being loved or at least special, I could not stomach a physical relationship with another man. I chose celibacy, which is not a bright prospect for an eighteen-year-old male.

One night I dreamed I saw a beautiful woman, semi-nude, lying on her back. I became sexually excited and was about to get close when a man stepped up and announced that it would cost me five dollars to sleep with her. I gave him the money, but woke up before I was able to touch her. I always wake up before. This is one of the major themes in my dreams. It's also an underlying nagging in my waking hours; natural impulses bucking the highly unnatural constraints of prison life. I try to suppress it as much as possible and to look at the positive side of celibacy; that, like a priest, I have traded the pleasures of the flesh for a more intense focus on the pleasure of the Spirit. But I assume the repressed urge leaks out sideways sometimes (as extra testosterone is prone to do) in the form of angry outbursts or physical agitation. This agitation has lessened with age. I am thankful to be in my fifties now, with only whispers of my previous testosterone levels. Men in the free world are taking pills to maintain their virility. I am happy that desire no longer haunts me so much.

But as much as I have yearned for sexual outlet, it is simple affection and loving touch that I miss and crave most deeply. It's an ache. I entered prison at an extreme deficit for affection. In years to come, the yearnings that came from being in my sexual prime and profoundly lonely would take their toll on me and for a time I had relationships with cross-dressing, effeminate men. We call it "forced bisexuality," because it is the closest we are able to get to the relationships we'd like to have. I am ashamed of these relationships, but it was what many inmates did in those days and desperate times are the impetus for desperate measures.

However at eighteen I had not yet reached that breaking point and the thought of intimacy with a man was repulsive. I had never had a girlfriend and it would be almost twenty years before I would have even a one-night stand with a woman.

Kim

It took me a couple of letters back and forth with Mickey before I learned that he has no access to a computer. Handwritten letters are the only way that he is able to communicate with the outside world. He has very tidy handwriting and sends long story-telling letters that only very rarely have a misspelled word or something scratched out. It's obvious he's been doing it for years while the rest of us dropped our pens in favor of keyboards and forgot how to move our hands in the particular way required of good penmanship.

Dear Kim,   10/1/11

Greetings and warm regards to you on this lovely Fall day. I sincerely hope this missive finds you well and in good health!

I received your letter concerning the advice on improving my manuscript, as well as an article for your magazine. These changes are enclosed with this letter, and I hope that you fully understand those that go into some more detail in my experiences at Granite. Let me know if there are questions.

Yes, you have my permission to re-edit it in whatever form you choose. I trust, from your letter, that you know exactly what you are doing.

No, we are not allowed computers here. In fact it was my uncle, out there, who translated it from long-hand to type-written. He also put it on floppy disc for me. I have since written him and asked that he mail the disc to you.

I type seventy-word-a-minute letters back to him, sometimes with my barely legible chicken scratch in the margins. He begins each letter with a greeting, often a couple sentences long and flowery. He usually takes time to include an inspiring quote or a poem he wrote. I say "hi" and then get right to business. His letters have the energy of an old man feeding the pigeons from a park bench. My letters are the obsessive jogger running circles around him.

I am accustomed to responses within minutes and rapid turnaround. For Mickey and me, each round of editing and writing can have a turnaround time of close to three weeks: about two weeks for a packet to get to him by US Mail and through prison security, a day for him to write his responses and several days for US Mail to bring them back to me. Working on this book with Mickey has taken me back to an earlier pace. It's a pace that allows ideas to sink deeply into consciousness, where they can germinate and grow. By the time I get Mickey's responses, I have harvested a whole crop of new ideas for us to play with. It's a good pace for me to re-learn. It's like taking deep breaths. It's also been an exercise in surrender. I have no control of this pace. There's absolutely nothing I can do to speed it up —and when I've felt impatient, which has been often, my "hurry up" energy has backfired on me, like hitting every red light when late for an appointment.

It has often happened that I will send Mickey a list of several questions and he will respond to one of them in beautiful detail. I will then wait two weeks to receive the rest of his answers, (during which time I will get regular letters from him with interesting new stories) only to get a letter saying, "So what do you need from me for the book?" I will then rewrite the four unanswered questions from the previous letter and wait another three weeks for his response. Deep breath. Surrender. Om.

If Mickey and I had been collaborating on this book using the typical 21st century modes of communication and technology, we'd have completed it in about a month. Doing it the maximum security prison way, it took us about eight months. If we'd gotten it done in a month, our collaboration would have simply been about a book-- and it didn't take us long to realize that this was about more than a book. In fact, the book may simply be a prop that brought us together for more important things. These eight months have been a crash course for us in something we have not yet been able to put a label to. The process has ripped away things we had been holding on to and given us something new to hold on to instead. It has been frustrating and fulfilling, distressing and comforting. Over and over again, it has caused us to question, dig deeper, take our consciousness higher to sort and figure things out. For example, several months into our collaboration a letter came from Mickey in which he expressed the highest praise for me. I promptly lost the letter. I had a hard time hearing what he had to say about me. I squirmed reading about how well he thought of me. The degree of my discomfort told me it was time to sit down and find the root of it.

Dear Mickey,
... I was writing [my husband] Jeff an email about you

yesterday and had one of those strong déjà vu moments that I've had occasionally while collaborating with you. I then vaguely remembered a dream I had at least a few years ago having to do with prison and a feather and suddenly knew that the dream had been about you. I thought I remembered saying to Jeff, ""Isn't it weird that I'd send a prison inmate a feather? I wonder what that means?" Little did I know that it wasn't metaphorical, but that I'd really be sending an inmate a feather. Sometimes I think I make these things up —and I'm sure I sometimes do!—so I asked Jeff if he remembered if I'd ever told him about a dream having to do with prison and a feather and he said that he did and that I had gone into detail about it. I was really moved by that dream —shaken up even. I think it may have been after that dream that I began looking into working in prisons, or volunteering in some way with inmates, but no jobs or positions ever quite fit my skills or interests. Mostly though, I was afraid of working in a prison, because I saw in my mind, not a minimum security prison working with women, but a maximum security prison working with men. No other population felt right —nothing else called to me —so I stopped trying to find something and waited for whatever it was that was calling to me to find me.

You said something along the lines of how amazingly kind I am to reach out to you the way that I do, but Mickey I am selfishly propelled to do what I do. Being connected with you and writing the book and finally walking down a path that has been calling to me for several years fills some big holes in me. This —all that "this" is —is for me a calling full-filled. I feel like a "connect the dots" in which the dots are finally being connected or a jigsaw puzzle that is being completed with some pieces that have been missing for a long time. Both of us have mentioned feeling like we have been taking steps in this direction our whole lives. What an odd pair we are. But as different as our lives look on the outside, we are very much alike, primarily because we are seekers and have the same general life missions. I'm so glad that you have come into my life or visa-versa and I look forward to what's next...

The phrase that stood out for me in his letter and for which I felt particularly squirmy was something about being the purest soul he's ever met. I realize that this is exactly the kind of thing that I sometimes say to him – in fact, at the time I received his letter, I had a letter in route to him saying that he was the most ego-less person I have ever known. I wonder if he reacts with as much discomfort as I do to these shining opinions of him. He goes through phases in which his letters are a little cooler in their emotional temperature. In those letters he'll often throw out details about himself that reflect his less savory past and his more shadowy side, like he's showing me that I'm wrong about him –or maybe testing to see if I still have the same positive review of him after learning more about who he "really" is. I do the very same thing. If we charted my letters with his I'm sure we'd see a pattern –a dance even –in which I take an emotional step forward or show him a little more of his magnificence and he takes a step back, then he takes an emotional step forward or shows me a little more of my magnificence and I take a step back. Over time our steps forward have gotten more strident and bold, while our steps back have remained about the same, so the dance is changing, but its rhythm still derives from a sense of unworthiness on both our parts.

R'Delle Anderson is a woman who does what she calls "soul readings." She offered me a free soul reading as a thank you for letting her use my art on her business materials. I had heard that she was gifted and so excitedly took her up on her offer. During the session I asked her what my purpose was in Mickey's life (She does not know who Mickey is and knows very little about me) and she said that I was to hold the light for Mickey, to hold the truth of who he really is, so that he could better hold the light and truth for others. That felt like a bull's-eye to me and I later wished that I had asked what Mickey's purpose was in my life –but then realized that I already knew. Mickey is --unknowingly and purely through example-- my sensei and I am his "Grasshopper." As I've gotten to know him, my reasons for not being as grateful, happy, content, faithful and peaceful as I'd like to be have been highlighted as the self-pitying, self-indulgent and wimpy excuses that they really are. If I were to sum up what I've learned from Mickey it would be, "If he can do it, then I have absolutely no excuses."

My friend Carter has an earth-bound, psychological theory on why Mickey and I feel such a strong connection. I sense that what she has to say on the matter is not only just as true as what R'Delle says, but encompasses his spiritual purpose in my life as well. Carter sees Mickey and I as much the same person with much the same background and much the same psychological reaction to our background. She sees the differences as simply a matter of scale. At first this sounded ludicrous, but then I got a flash of the therapy groups I used to lead and received some insight into how this could be the case for Mickey and me.

The "Penny Game" was an icebreaker I used in my therapy groups. Most of my groups were for survivors of abuse, so there were more than the usual trust issues to overcome. In order to feel comfortable sharing and baring their souls, my clients needed to know that they were among people who would understand them. If they got empathy that was icing on the cake, but most simply wanted to avoid the abuse of being misunderstood. The Penny Game was designed to show my group's members that they were in the company of people who would understand them.

Each member of the group was given a pile of pennies. They were then instructed to go around the circle three times, each time disclosing something that was a little more personal and risky. When someone made a disclosure, the others in the group would give that person a penny if they related to the disclosure in any way. For example, a group member might say, "I am divorced." If anyone in the group had ever felt failure in a relationship or mourned the loss of a love, or a dream, or dealt with the upheavals of a major life change, they would put a penny in that person's pile and explain how they could relate to that person's experience. It was very rare that someone failed to find a way to relate to another's experience.

On the surface, Mickey's life and mine couldn't look more different. For example, Mickey is a three-strike inmate serving a life sentence. I have a traffic violation from 1987. Mickey's parents were drug addicts. My parents had the same liquor in the liquor cabinet my entire childhood —until high school that is, when my friends and I poured ourselves swigs and then replaced the missing liquid with water. But like the Penny Game, our vastly different experiences had similar themes running through them that required similar coping skills –and produced in us similar neuroses, rebellions and drives.

Mickey and I are part of a global tribe of soul brothers and sisters. We are linked by the fact that we began the emotional and/or logistical responsibilities of adulthood very early. Some of us experienced an abrupt halt to childhood due to a traumatic event or loss. Others had families or communities that were abusive, neglectful, emotionally or financially ill equipped, or God bless them, all the above. Whatever the case, we missed out on some of the qualities and experiences that define childhood. We didn't believe in things like tooth fairies and Santa Claus. We did things we didn't want to do. By "Things we didn't want to do," I'm not referring to math homework and mowing the lawn. I'm talking about *real* character building things like raising siblings or ourselves, taking beatings, performing sexual acts, being the family maid and cook, or worse, the family psychotherapist. We were catapulted into adulthood.

The members of this fraternity are often identifiable by the fact that we spend our adult lives avoiding doing things we don't want to do. We figure we made that quota early. Those in relationship with us often call us "control freaks," a label that is often accurate and fair. As a young adult, I was always the designated driver. I didn't like to drink much anyway (because I didn't like being out of control), but the main reason I drove was that I wanted to be in control of the getaway car. I wanted to be able to leave should things go awry. As a college student, I knew the only way I'd learn a foreign language would be to live in a foreign country. But I couldn't make myself do a semester abroad. I was too afraid I'd be stuck in a place I didn't want to be, doing things I didn't want to do.

We rebel against authority, either subtly or blatantly, because we learned that those who make the rules and set social guidelines don't always make them with the common good in mind. We learned early that adults can be wrong, that their judgment is often obscured by their emotional baggage and faulty world views. In response to this knowledge we either began relying on an internal compass for guidance or gave up on guidance altogether, both external and internal, and simply began drifting, going where the wind blew us. Mickey and I are, by and large, drifters.

While many of us were taught in Sunday school that God takes care of us and protects us, that hadn't been our experience, so we lost trust in both organized religion and God. Most of us saw God as having done a botch job on our childhoods and so decided that we, more than God, knew what was best for us. Some of us became atheists, relying on the "facts" to inform and direct us. Others in our tribe started at the base of the mountain of rubble that was our faith and for some unfathomable reason began rebuilding with an almost single-minded intensity. This latter course is the one that Mickey and I have taken. We have been so consumed with understanding the role and reasoning of God in our lives that spirituality has become the most defining aspect of our characters.

Many of us is this tribe are allergic to careers or any

kind of commitment-bound employment. This type of committed works falls under the category of "not wanting to be stuck doing something we don't want to do." I may be more allergic to employment than most. I was so late in declaring a college major (over a year past the deadline) that the school required me to write an essay about why I was so late declaring my major before they'd accept my paperwork. After I made my declaration, I continued to agonize over my choice throughout the entirety of my higher education, which lasted a total of almost nine years.

When I say I'm allergic to work, I literally mean that I'm allergic to work. I began my first full-time career employment at the age of twenty-three, two weeks out of graduate school. I was healthy as a horse in grad school and for the twenty-one years prior. I even managed to get through grad school without developing a caffeine habit. But as soon as I started working, I had such severe allergies that I missed whole days of work and had to begin allergy shots. All day long, I would sneeze so loudly and violently that everyone in the office would jump. My coworkers began to get nervous disorders. The office manager got tired of saying "Bless you," all day and so each morning would make one sign of the cross to last the whole day. As for caffeine, I was mainlining it within two weeks of starting the job and super-charging its boost with candy. I was attempting to recreate the zest and energy I had previously felt toward life, when life had looked wide open, bright and unconstrained.

I managed to work for other people for about five years before venturing out on my own. I did very well in my private psychotherapy practice, but spent much of that time getting an MBA so that I could change careers. I had no idea what I was going to change *to*. I simply needed to know that I'd have a ticket to something different than where I was. Even with other career possibilities in mind, I became progressively more depressed. One day I decided to give up, not only on a career in psychotherapy, but on the world of careers entirely. When my former boss learned that I wasn't renewing my counseling certification she was appalled. I told her that I'd rather waitress than do even one more hour of counseling –and that's exactly what I've done, along with a smattering of career-related positions throughout, like grant writing, workshops and event planning, but *always* on a contract or freelance basis. I haven't wanted, ever again, to be locked into something.

These days I am an artist, a freelance editor and on occasion I do some freelance writing as well. I also publish an online magazine (www.loveyourlifemagazine.com) in which life coaches and other luminaries provide inspiration and tips on happy healthy living. I am proud of the type of work that I do as well as its quality and the variety keeps me engaged and interested. But nothing has ever hit the spot for me or held as much meaning as this book with Mickey. I feel like I am walking the path that I was born to walk, doing the work that I was born to do and the path is evolving as I walk it.

The paths that Mickey and I have walked up until now have been vastly different due primarily to one element: expectation. My inner circle has had high expectations of me and I have done my best to live up to them. People have expected little of Mickey or have expected the worst from him and he has lived down to those expectations. People haven't believed in Mickey and so Mickey hasn't believed in Mickey. To a degree, I have been able to see myself through the eyes of the people who believe in me and so have never fallen to the socio-economic depths to which Mickey has fallen. Mickey, who is the more gifted of the two of us, has been given few reasons to try --and some pretty solid reasons not to.

It could be said that neither of us have lived up to our potential --in Mickey's case this *would* be said -- but it could also be said that we have lived up to another kind of potential, and perhaps the kind for which we were born. Mickey and I see Life and Spirit differently than most people and often those around us tend to shift a little, to step outside their boxes and experience Life a little differently along with us. I don't know what you would call this role and maybe there's not a name for it --yet --but whatever it is that we are doing, it feels purposeful and we do it naturally and well.

It is not characteristic of all the members of our tribe, but Mickey and I, along with many of us have learned to see that people are not black or white, but a wide spectrum with many shades of gray. We have learned to sec the good in people who have been bad to us. We have learned to understand the pain from which bad deeds spring and have seen that under the wounds, at the core, is love. We have learned compassion--and compassion has been a springboard for forgiveness. We are alike in so many ways, but it is our ability to see the good in people who are being bad that probably most impacts our day-to-day lives and our life missions. I believe that this, more than anything else that we brought forth from our childhoods, is the driving mechanism behind our life purposes.

Another identifying characteristic of our global fraternity is that we either collect or avoid things that depend on us. Early adulthood survivors tend to be crazy cat ladies, going way over the legal pet limit, or mentally and physically allergic to anything requiring care. It depends which way our trapeze swings. What we have in common is that our trapezes tend to swing in wide arcs, far away from the care-giving norm. I once got angry at my potted hibiscus because it needed water every single day. Every. Single. Day. –which tells you which way my trapeze has swung. Mickey's tendencies in this area are harder to measure, because he's spent most of his life in prison, but his stories allude to a tendency to collect people to care for, both on the street and in prison. He seems always on the lookout for ways to help. His caretaking trapeze seems to have swung the opposite direction from mine. If he had lived his life as a free man, with people believing in him, he'd probably be something like a hospice worker, a drug rehab counselor –or a prison clergyman. He – the half of our duo who is in prison for life –is considerably nicer and less self-absorbed than I am.

Many say that parenting is the hardest job in the world and even the happiest mothers I know feel like they're busting out of jail when they get a moment away from the kids. But for those of us who lose our minds when put in a situation from which we feel we can't escape, the lifetime commitment to the monumentally challenging and often uncomfortable role of parenting is in many ways our worst nightmare come true. We become like trapped animals and at times are willing to chew off our legs to free ourselves.

Over and over again we hear about women who did a "Kramer vs. Kramer," lost their minds and left their children. I can guarantee that each and every one of those moms was an early childhood survivor. All reason escapes us when we're trapped like that. Like the Vietnam vet who curls up in a fetal position when a car backfires, the inescapability of our parenting responsibilities triggers every emotion having to do with the inescapability of our childhoods and —as we did in childhood —we detach mentally and emotionally. In time, some of us become so detached that we are no longer cognizant of the consequences of our actions and unknowingly sound the death knell on our emotional and social wellbeing by leaving our families or just mentally and emotionally checking out.

I love my children, but in the inescapability of my role as mother I have paced like a caged cat and experienced a restlessness that borders on —and sometimes surpasses —the level of explosive. Being a mother has triggered every raw nerve and each of those nerves leads to the birthplace of each and every one of my issues. I do not like being trapped.

Mickey and I have been placed in situations from which we cannot readily escape. This has thrown us to an emotional and mental rock bottom, a place in which we have had to face it all —and as Janice Joplin (another early childhood survivor) so wisely sang, "Freedom's just another way of saying 'nothing left to lose'." In our inescapable situations, Mickey and I have discovered the true meaning of freedom.

The Blues

On the thirty-fifth day in Receiving I was ordered to appear before a committee in the Captain's Office. They informed me that I was being assigned to a cell in F-Cell house and a job in the prison print shop. I was dismissed and told to pack my stuff. I would be moving that day. Although I felt some anxiety –more than some, really—the overriding feeling I had was one of finally belonging somewhere, of being part of something. This feeling faded over the years and I feel incredibly sad when I look back at the teenage version of me who needed to go to prison to find a place to belong, but on that day, I felt a sense of having arrived.

F-Cell house was one of the newer cell houses, built in about the 1940's. It was designed with four tiers, with cells facing one another across a wide corridor, or 'Run,' that ran straight down the center. I was assigned to a four-man cell, but there were only two occupants; Peewee and Hoppy. Like me, they were both a little quiet and reserved. They too were in prison for armed robbery, but in prison, you never ask a man what he's in for, you ask "What did they say you did?" This gives the person the opportunity to circumvent the truth if he chooses. Being in prison is punishment enough. No one wants to punish themselves further by thinking about the mistakes they've made; what they did that landed them there. This is a courteous way to ask the question.

Once Pee Wee and Hoppy ascertained that I wasn't a sex offender, they were more open and welcoming. Inmates convicted of sex crimes did not fare well in general population. Most voluntarily went into protective custody or risked being abused or murdered by an outraged fellow inmate, especially one who had children.

In the code and subculture of prison life, sexual predators are subjected to the same basic treatment and stereotypes as they are everywhere. For the most part, they are ostracized and unwelcome on the yard. I've often wondered if there isn't more to the downgrading of sexual predators than simply being outraged at the abuse of children. My experience has been that racists and bullies tend to be people who need to see someone else as lower than them in order to feel better about themselves. Those of us in prison are about as low as people can get in the social hierarchy. We ARE the bottom of the social ladder. I think we designate a certain in-house category as being lower than us to achieve this same purpose –we may be low, but we're not as low as THEM.

Another part of the shunning of sexual predators has never quite balanced out in my mind. There are plenty of us in prison with anger management issues and most of us have drug abuse issues too. Put the two together and a fair percentage of us have hurt a child in one way or another. I wonder if, just as those who are latent homosexuals tend to be the ones who degrade and hurt homosexuals, the sexual predators in our midst cause us to face our own deviancy, our own tendencies toward the immoral. We want to shun, beat down and even kill that part of ourselves –but instead project those feelings onto those who weren't able to control their impulses and who let the monster loose.

But these thoughts and questions came much later in my prison career. Entering the corrections system at eighteen, I didn't think this deeply. I didn't question much. I simply worked to survive. In prison, survival is dependent upon learning and conforming to the rules of prison management and more importantly, the unwritten rules and social conventions of the inmates. We have a "pirate's code" so to speak and those who do not follow it are either marooned or walk the metaphorical plank.

I have never had the confidence to be outgoing. I am quiet and introverted. Socially, I have been the equivalent of wallpaper. In prison this proved to be a personality well suited to survival. I had very few friends and was mostly a loner. I was afraid of groups. This was good, because when you belong to a group in prison, you do their bidding, which can include killing someone. I was a quiet observer and in this way, learned the ropes and rules. I remained as invisible as possible.

My first morning in F-cell house, I was awakened at dawn by an inmate who ran a stick across the bars of every cell. This was our daily wake-up call and made us miss the buzzing alarm clocks that most of us had found so annoying in the free world.

Following breakfast, I reported to the shower/clothing room. This was where I got my issue of 'blues': blue jeans and blue shirts, along with my white underclothing. They sewed my number on each shirt and pant and had me discard my coveralls in a dirty clothes bin.

Striding out on the yard in my new uniform, I felt a curious sense of hubris: I was now an official convict, with my very own prison number stitched on everything, just like in the movies. I felt a sense of identity and belonging that had been lacking on the outside. Maybe this feeling came from a lower place, a place in which I felt a match between my sad surroundings and my level of worthiness. But maybe it came from a higher level, a place in which I knew that prison wasn't just where I'd serve time, but where I'd serve a purpose.

Discarded

My sister Teresa and I were seated in an office building of the State Welfare Department. I was seven and my sister, nine. My mother was there, among several men dressed in suits and ties. Mom reached down and kissed Teresa and then walked out the door. We began to cry and begged the men to let us go with her, but they restrained us. I poked my head out the door and watched her walk rapidly down a corridor, sobbing. My thoughts were that she was throwing us away, much as one would a worn-out article of clothing. I thought we had done something bad and I wanted to die. We were being placed in a Foster Home while she went away to treat a drug addiction. I had been happy at home and because I was so young, was not aware of my mom's drug use or that drugs were a problem. I did not understand why our mom was leaving us behind. I thought we were not good enough to deserve parents. My father was serving time. We had no one.

Teresa and I were placed in a foster home together. Our foster mother was abusive and we huddled together for emotional support. It was a miserable time for us and we began to lose hope of ever again feeling safe or happy. In the backyard of the foster home was a swing set. I walked back there one day and found Teresa sitting motionless on the swing, her dark red hair shining in the sun with a sparkle that didn't fit the mood of the scene. I came to her and saw that she was weeping. She looked at me with her dark, soulful eyes and cried, "Oh Mickey, I want to go home." My young heart was breaking for her. I too wanted to go home.

Teresa and I were very close. It was the two of us

40

against the world for most of our childhood. We were all the other had. We were so close that if she cried, I cried and if she laughed I would look for the same humor.

After a little over a year in foster care my mom was stable enough to parent again and took my sister and I back to live with her. My mom had very recently remarried, so she and my step-dad came to pick us up and bring us back home. Seeing her again and knowing that I was going home was one of the happiest days of my life. I felt a rush of relief and happiness that was overwhelming. It was like getting out of prison.

My stepfather was very good to us. He too was hooked on drugs (he overdosed on heroin in the late 1980s) but he improved upon our little family unit with his gentleness and sense of humor. He used to take us to the bar with him (back when people weren't too concerned about children being in bars) and he'd banter happily with the bartender and with us. I was fascinated with the mixing of drinks and how people would take a sip of their newly created concoction and exclaim to the bartender that it was "perfect." Bartenders seemed to have the ability to make people happy and I decided that when I came of age, I would be a bartender.

Initiation by Fire

The prison Print Shop was in a two-story building across from male clothing and above me on the upper floor was the broom & mattress factory. It was my first day on the job, July 27, 1973; a date full of such mayhem and violence that it is still clearly etched into my consciousness.

Upon reporting for work that morning, an assistant supervisor assigned me the simple task of binding covers on Department of Corrections manuals. I was seated at a long wooden table near a window that faced the Lieutenant's Office. Next to me was a convict with both arms under the table. He was shooting up narcotic drugs. I quickly looked away. What was not my business was not my business. This is part of the convict code. (A quick word about the convict code; it has five tenets, or laws, that a good convict does not break. 1. Do not snitch; 2. Pay your debts; 3. Show respect; 4. No sex crimes; and 5. Do your own time. By following these rules one generally pulled easier time and gained respect.)

An hour of work passed. Then two. I was rapidly falling into the groove and lost in the hypnotic rhythm of the task. The trance was shattered by an announcement over the PA system that echoed across the yard. A slurring voice blared "This is a revolution. We're taking over this place!" I did not know how to react. But I knew the PA system was located in the Lieutenant's Office, so I determined that this was no bullshit, this was for real.

I scrambled to the window and with mounting anxiety,

watched as several inmates pushed a wheelbarrow down the ramp and toward the hospital. In the wheelbarrow was a captain, with his upper torso covered in blood. I later discovered that he had been beaten by the drunken inmates.

Shortly after the announcement, several convicts with torches surrounded the Print Shop. "You guys come out of there!" one of them shouted. "We're gonna burn it down!"

One of the guards told them that the door was locked and the rioting inmates went to work on it with hammers and hatchets. It did not take long before it crashed in.

The inmates in the shop hurried out, I along with them. As I left, I looked back at the cowering staff locked in the office. I knew they would become hostages. I hoped they would live through it.

Outside, the yard was total chaos. Two thousand men ran around like ants on an anthill that had been kicked, some carrying torches, most carrying weapons. There were fires everywhere. At times the smoke caused my eyes to water and I could not see.

The print shop, broom & mattress factory, laundry, book bindery, furniture factory and chapel were all in flames. We had radios on the yard and could monitor the news as the riot went forth. We heard the Governor's Press Secretary say, "The animals have taken over the zoo." We heard a lot of words being spoken and a lot of judgments being made, but nothing was being done. The Governor fiddled while his prison burned.

Through the smoke I could see fights and bludgeoning. This was a window of opportunity for inmates to settle old scores and animosities. I saw an inmate shot in the abdomen by a tower guard perched atop the wall. I resolved to keep away from the towers and as far as possible from the melee.

I found Hoppy, my cellmate, sitting on a bench far to the sidelines with several other inmates, quietly drinking pruno from a bucket with a tin cup (pruno is an alcoholic concoction made from fermented oranges). We sat and watched the chaos and no one said much. None of us would admit our fears – admitting fear is simply not done in prison-- but the atmosphere around the bench was crackling with suppressed anxiety. I too sat and drank, staying as invisible as possible while waiting for the calming effect of the pruno to kick in. I drained the first few tin cups in one gulp. I was quickly intoxicated. With rage on the loose all around me, intoxicated was exactly where I wanted to be.

Hoppy and the others were armed with clubs and knives. I asked where I might find a weapon in case I needed to defend myself.

"Go to the back of the mess hall, to the butcher shop", Hoppy instructed, "You'll find something there."

I found a cutting knife half the length of my arm and stuck it through the belt loops of my pants, like a scabbard. It remained there for the course of the riot.

A few hours after finding the shank, I discovered the canteen building, complete with groceries and smokes. It had two sales windows, and the inmates who worked in the shop were shoving out canned goods, pastries, and beverages to anyone who asked for them.

A wheelbarrow was nearby. I knew it might be a long time before the prison was retaken. I filled the wheelbarrow with food items and wheeled it all the way up to our cell. The cell doors were open because the locking mechanism had been ripped out and rendered ineffective. It would be many months before they were repaired.

I went through each motion and movement of that day like a robot. The shock of the violence, the smoke and even the sudden lack of constraint and relative freedom rendered me almost emotionless. Even intoxicated, I felt more machine than man. I've now learned that this mental state is called "dissociation" and happens when circumstances are too uncomfortable to handle directly. After having already spent years in the Juvenile Corrections system, you'd think I'd have been accustomed to violence. Violence had become part of my life and I had learned to expect it, but I don't believe anyone ever really acclimates to it. We continue to feel horror and fear, but instead of experiencing it, we bury the feelings well below consciousness –where they fester and boil and eventually cause a whole lot of trouble. In my case, that trouble manifested itself as murder.

Tighter Than a Clamshell

It was 1967. I was eleven years old and the juvenile justice system had placed me in the hands of a "Christian School," set in the northern back-country hills of Oklahoma.

My parents and I had a good relationship, but I felt the pull to get in trouble because I I just wanted to stand out in some way. This particular time, I had been caught stealing and it was the court's belief that with some strict religious character, I might be saved from myself, so it was to a Christian school that they sent me.

My parents came to visit once, but the staff at the school was so hostile to them that they never again returned. I was there three months before I ran away. I was caught the next day in Muskogee, Oklahoma, after telephoning a friend in Oklahoma City to come get me. Instead of getting me, he'd called the police. Back at the Christian School, I was berated by the superintendent for my sinful disregard of God's Authority. He slapped my face several times and shouted angrily that I came from a "family of parasites," and that I would never amount to anything. He then dismissed me and ordered that I report to my cottage "father" to pray and ask forgiveness.

I did not pray, nor did I report back to my cottage for another beating. I ran to the highway and hitchhiked my way to nowhere in particular, hoping to bump into something good somewhere. But the world was mean and I didn't want more of the meanness to seep into me, so I shut myself up tighter than a clamshell. When you're shut up that tight, no good can seep in either.

Cruel and Unusual Punishment

It was late afternoon and shadows were lengthening across the yard. The riot had kicked off early that morning. The presence of the hostages kept the guards and police at bay; they would not storm the prison before the hostages were freed and safe. There were at least thirty of them, one of whom was the Deputy Warden. Several inmates, armed with weapons, escorted them across the yard from time to time. They were guarding them from inmates as well as using them as a bargaining chip. Some of the more violent inmates wanted to snuff them in an act of vengeance.

My clothing had darkened with soot from the many fires that were raging. I resolved to head for male clothing and change into clean ones. The authorities had cut the power to the prison, so light was dim in the clothing and shower room and it was difficult to make out objects. I heard a man pleading. Peering closer, I saw four inmates in a state of undress, with a fifth kneeling before them. He was performing oral sex between his pleas that his life be spared.

I ascertained that I had a better place to be for the moment and hastily took my leave.

Later in the evening I passed the clothing room and saw how that drama had ended. The inmate who had pleaded was on the ground, face down. His bare back was littered with stab wounds. He was quite dead.

I was shaken by what I saw. I quickly made my way to another part of the yard, and understood for the first time how real all of this was; a life could be taken at someone's whim.

Suddenly, my pride in being a convict vanished, and I wanted only to get away, to run somewhere, but there was no place to go. The riot lasted three horrible days.

Finally, the negotiators, including the warden, met with a council of inmates and promised that conditions at the prison would improve. After this, the hostages were released.

The improvements never happened, of course. The authorities were only concerned with the safe release of the hostages. They would have agreed to fly us to Cuba, if requested. It was naïve to think otherwise. After the riot things got worse. Much worse.

They stormed the prison soon thereafter; Highway Patrol Troopers, Deputy Sheriffs, local Cops and the National Guard. They steered an easy thousand of us at gunpoint onto one of the yards. They then drove in a tank, set up a barricade around the tank and trained its cannon on us. I kept my distance.

July was a scorching hot month. But it was the nights that alarmed me. That was when I became most vigilant. I heard and saw people getting shanked. I witnessed a young black kid charging across the yard with several black inmates chasing him. He was trying to make it to the barricade but did not. He fell over a table and his pursuers caught up with him. They smashed in his head with a hatchet, and he died, face-down.

The cops did nothing. They were dispassionate of the violence. They were there as a show of force and would not intervene unless it was one of their own being slashed to pieces.

We were kept on the yard for two more days without food or medical care for the inmates who were wounded. I had an epileptic seizure that went unnoticed —or at least untended.

On the third day we were marched into the East Cell House. The cell doors could not be opened mechanically so they rigged a system in which the doors could be opened and closed manually.

Three of us were placed into two-man cells. We had no blankets or mattresses, and we rotated so that each person took a turn sleeping on the cement floor, while the other two slept on a bed frame.

We were not issued soap or toilet paper for the first week, so we used the brown paper bags that our food arrived in to clean ourselves.

Ten days later they removed one man from each cell and placed him in a double cell with one other occupant. We were also issued one mattress and wool blanket per man—still no sheets, but at least we had something with which to keep us warm. It was one of the few comforts given to us over the next two years.

We were fed sparingly; two simple sack lunches per day. Men were losing weight rapidly. We were hungry for two years.

Out of frustration we would shake and rattle our doors until the noise would become deafening. The sound spread for miles, we were told.

In response to the rebellion, the guards would bring in a machine that put out a fog of tear gas. The gas burned our eyes, nose, and throat, and many of the older cons would pass out and have to be carried away. But it did not bring quiet to the tiers. It only ratcheted up the decibel level.

I grew to hate my captors and their insidious torture machine. One day the Warden was spat on by an inmate. In retaliation for this, fire hoses were dragged down the run and each inmate was hit with a high-pressure spear of water. The water knocked me to the floor and rolled me to the back wall. Nothing was spared the soaking. My family photos were ruined and floated out to the run. There was a photo of me in a cowboy hat at about the age of two, being held by my pretty teenage mother. I would look at that photo when I needed a reminder that I had been loved. It was washed away. Our blankets, mattresses and clothing were drenched. It was February in Oklahoma and they opened the windows on the outside tiers so that we shook and shivered in the wet until well into the following day.

The Not So Great Escape

I believe in angels. I was once stranded on a San Diego bench at two o'clock in the morning, penniless. The wind off the ocean made me shiver all the way through. Suddenly a fellow drove up in a blue pick-up truck and stopped. He got out and said to me that the Angels would not let him sleep that night. They told him "someone needed help," and he said matter-of-factly that I must be the one. I soon ascertained that he was neither gay nor psychotic and accepted his help, although as cold as I was I would probably have accepted it even had he been either of the two. He drove me to a place where I had friends and then drove away. I thanked this good man and the angels in solemn prayer.

In 1975, a couple years after the riot, I believe the Angels once more intervened in my life.

They called me to present myself to the Classification Committee. They had reviewed my case and figured that because I was brought out of receiving and into the prison only a couple of days before the riot's eruption, it was unlikely that I was a willing participant and should therefore qualify for a lower security facility.

I was elated. Not only because I would be escaping the tear gas but because escape itself might prove possible. After two years I had had more than enough of my prison number and desperately wanted freedom. I was not yet twenty years old.

"Into the forest dark and deep,
I have promises to keep,
And miles to go before I sleep"
- Robert Frost

Stringtown Correctional Center (SCC) overlooks Lake Atoka in the southeast corner of Oklahoma. It is surrounded by double fences topped with razor wire and gun towers a few hundred yards apart.

Inside, the inmates live in dormitories – or did in 1975. Most everyone worked. I was assigned to the blood plasma center. In those days cons could donate a pint of blood plasma twice a week. They would receive five dollar's worth of canteen tickets per pint. It was a simple and easy way to make money, with no ill-health effects to the donor.

My job was to go from bed to bed, monitoring the flow of saline solutions that dripped into the tube, keeping the lines open. I would also change the blood bags once they were full. Being able to work and move around was the closest to satisfaction that I had felt in a long while, but it was short lived because the government said the job was taking unfair advantage of inmates and so it was shut down. Vocational programs were offered to the inmates, but I had no motivation to learn a trade or in any way better myself. I simply wanted out.

Six months after my arrival at Stringtown, I eased out the unlocked door of the dorm at two o'clock in the morning. It was pure foolishness, but I had an irresistible urge to run. For me, prison wasn't so much about being locked away from the rest of the world. It was about being locked in with myself. In the free world, I had run from my problems and emotions through drugs and alcohol. Others in the free world run from their problems by moving to another city or changing relationships or jobs or in any way staying very busy. In prison, there is nowhere to run, very little to do, very few distractions and limited drugs and alcohol to deal with this fact. I was determined to run away from the feelings that were haunting me and get to the free world where distraction and drugs were everywhere --or die trying.

My friend David had given me a handful of coins and the telephone number of his cousin if I could make it to a telephone on the "outside." My intention was to hop the freight train that roared by the prison about once an hour. I had watched and observed for several months, and decided that the early hours of the morning would be the best time to attempt an exit from that place.

I made my way to the first fence, directly under a tower. I went unnoticed.

I removed my dark army jacket and threw it over the razor wire, scaled the fence and slid easily over, touching down in a meadow. I was still spotlighted by the lights coming from the fence, though the dark meadow lay only a few feet away.

From a tower about one hundred yards away came rounds of gunfire. The grass around my feet flew about in tufts and I was hit in the right thigh. I was knocked to the ground and felt panic as the firing increased. I crawled into the dark pasture and the firing ceased. Relief.

I touched my leg and it came away bloody. But I did not believe it was serious, more of a flesh wound. Still, I tore a sleeve from my shirt and used it as a tourniquet. I raised myself to my feet and discovered that I could still walk, but running was out of the question. It was not long before I heard the baying of the bloodhounds. They had themselves a rabbit. But the game was not yet over.

I crossed the highway to the railroad tracks where a train was coming, fast. Alas, it was coming too fast. I couldn't run fast enough to safely jump and feared that if I grabbed a ladder it would be my undoing. It passed me by. Opportunity missed.

Dejected and with the hounds closing in, I sat on the tracks and rolled a cigarette. The dogs soon arrived and made sure I didn't move. It was not long before a Captain and some State Troopers arrived. "Well, boy," the Captain smiled, "You ain't even run two miles." I showed him my bullet wound and he was taken aback. No one knew I had been hit, not even the tower guard who shot me.

I was 'cuffed and placed in the Highway Patrol car and driven to a hospital, where they mended my leg. From there it was back to Oklahoma State Penitentiary and the Hole. I would not see a lower security prison again for eight years.

I pled guilty to escape and received two more years to run consecutively with the twenty-five that I was already serving. I imagined that I would get shanked or die of a disease and never again see the free world. I now looked at life through dark and distorted lenses. I was becoming institutionalized.

Kim

Most of my life's major decisions have been based on an avoidance of having anyone or anything dependent upon me or to be obligated in any way. In fact, the only reason that I married (besides the fact that I love him and he asked) was because my husband is so incredibly self-contained and utterly un-dependent. For the first three years of our marriage we lived six hundred miles apart and that was okay with us. I was also highly ambivalent about children and leaned toward not having them, but Life had other plans for me and (ten years into my marriage, at the age of forty) perfectly orchestrated a day of temporary insanity with ovulation that resulted in twins. The highest maintenance pet that I myself have chosen was a beta fish. After a few years I gave him away because he was spending more time with his fish-sitter (while I traveled) than with me. I've moved twenty seven times since my eighteenth birthday. I like change. I like newness. I like starting fresh. I like not getting too involved or going too deep—at least not for too long.

I came out of my childhood with some beautiful life lessons and life skills, but healthy boundaries weren't among them. I have historically divulged too quickly, trusted too completely and redrawn the line of chalk until there was no healthy distance between another and me. Put succinctly, I have been a doormat and my unflagging trust has made it so that I have often been used, manipulated and conned—"conned" being an operative word in relation to Mickey. After a few decades of boundary-less relationships, I swung the other direction into over-cautiousness and over-guardedness. I became a bit of a recluse –a very outgoing, gregarious and socially adept recluse, but a recluse nonetheless. My more than typical need for solitude fit my budding life as an artist and writer, so I assumed that I was simply evolving into the typical lifestyle of creative types —a life with lots of room to think and create. To some extent, I'm sure this is the case, but I'm just as sure that part of it is that in solitude I don't have to deal with the risks and messes of relationships. In solitude I can relax, let down my guard and rest.

While I am very friendly and open on a surface level, I am slow to open more deeply and even slower to jump into a friendship. With Mickey's inmate status, chemical abuse history and criminal record, it took me significantly longer to let down my guard and even longer to get over my anxiety about becoming one of those women who gets suckered into becoming a sugar mama to an inmate. I spent the first two or three months of our collaboration scrutinizing his letters for signs self-entitlement, lack of conscience, dishonesty, craziness or milder forms of instability. Despite the fact that I had read his manuscript and felt the soulfulness and heart in his words, I trusted neither Mickey nor myself. This hypersensitivity was heightened by the fact that almost no one else trusted Mickey either. What they knew about him was that he was a con with a long criminal record. The jury was still out on him, so to speak.

Eventually it occurred to me that Mickey probably felt just as vulnerable as I did. I was holding the life of his book in my hands. This book is the one thing Mickey has. It's his baby, his contribution to Life. He doesn't have the means or the wherewithal to get it published on his own and had to put it into the hands of a stranger. I may be gullible, but Mickey has been in prison for the most part since 1973. Of the two of us, I am more worldly and subsequently, the more capable of manipulating. While I was gulping with anxiety about sending money to his prison account, he was probably gulping with anxiety over the business arrangement I was proposing, not to mention the fact that he really wasn't certain that I knew what I was doing. I was a lifeline that had been thrown to him, but was this lifeline connected to anything solid? Even I didn't know the answer to that question.

As our relationship has progressed, we have both leaned little by little into trusting –trusting the other and more importantly, trusting the Life Force that brought us together and the plan that It has for us. However, for me, and I would assume for Mickey too, our trust issues have layers and there is much for us to look at and process.

I have more than a couple personalities and each has different interests and a short attention span. I like starting things and creating things, but lose interest when it comes to maintaining things. Behind me is a trail of projects and creations that were started with gusto, but then hastily finished with underwhelming fanfare, abandoned or handed over to another. In general, I have been okay with this way of skipping through the world because it has produced more benefit than harm –but this isn't the case when what I'm abandoning is not a project, but a person. Mickey has made his quota on abandonment in this lifetime and my propensity to swirl in, do my thing and leave made me more than a little nervous. I am well aware that my role in Mickey's life is not temporary. He is not a residence from which I can move, a beta fish I can hand over to someone else. He is not a "flavor of the month." He is a man who is looking for bright spots in an otherwise bleak existence.

In my young adulthood, most of my relationships were with soul-full, generous boys with big wounded hearts and exceptionally deep dark streaks. For example, there was the boyfriend who would hold a loaded gun to my head when I'd push the right buttons. Mickey's strong resemblance to this personality profile pushed my own particular buttons, among them the panic button. In fact, Mickey's last crime –his third strike and the crime for which he ultimately got a life sentence –was so similar to an altercation I'd had with my boyfriend, knife and all, that I knew this was no coincidence. Life was telling me there was work for me to do here and I knew that with that work would come healing. But the fear I felt about how this "work" would show up was not small.

In the beginning, this was all about a book. It was a business arrangement –not a friendship-- not at all-- just an "arrangement." I would help Mickey write and publish his book. It would be meaningful. It would be interesting. I would be helpful. Then I would be on my way.

My letters to Mickey started out as multiple pages of questions, directives and changes awaiting his approval. But somewhere in each stack of task-mastering there would usually be a little something personal, the tiniest morsel of non-business related subject matter. Mind you, as the weeks went on I wrote many paragraphs of more personal and friendly material to him. I just didn't send them. I deleted those paragraphs until I felt comfortable with what was on the page. For the first several months, my comfort zone was somewhere around four sentences of rather benign personal details. In fact, I didn't so much talk about myself as about my kids, deep disclosures like; "Ben was a samurai for Halloween and Eliza was a robot."

Increasingly, Mickey honed in on the teeny tiny personal morsels that I sent and made a point of responding to them and asking a question or two. If I said, "Eliza started an art class," he would respond with "How does Eliza like her art class?" He would use anything personal that I offered to take one gentle step forward. It was like coaxing a bird to eat out of his hand, which is something I bet he could do. He never asked a question without me first bringing up the topic and even then, kept questions in the safe and comfortable range.

While Mickey has been treating me like the skittish bird that I am, I've been coming at him with a crow bar, prying into every corner of his psyche. I am by nature a psychotherapist and am inclined to ask overly-personal questions, but my role as his editor gave me license to ask even more brazen questions than I normally would. I asked him questions about his intimate life before and since prison. I asked him about his relationship with God. I asked him if he feels loved. I asked him how he feels about himself. I asked him to unbury memories from a past that is full of pain and regret. I asked him about his heartbreak. I asked him to look at how he feels about spending the rest of his days in a home of concrete, steel and confinement.

This is a guy who has spent almost his whole life in a system where feelings are not shown or acknowledged, where they are stuffed deep below consciousness. He lives in a world where staying away from the past is the least painful option. That's where I've gone with my crow bar. I asked him how he felt –how he *really* felt – during every painful and positive event and challenge of his life and I tell him to write these feelings down. The feelings he's unearthed are now in this book for anyone to see. God bless Mickey, not only because he's in a maximum security prison for life, but because he's had me helping him with his book.

Mickey has handled my deep probing with grace. He has answered my questions forthrightly and without complaint –and if his answers don't go deeply enough for me, he willingly takes himself yet further into the memories and pain ---That is, except when he doesn't-- - Mind you, he hasn't complained, but he hasn't always answered my questions or given me the stories I want either. For example, I asked him at least fifteen questions regarding life at Pleasant Valley, questions like, "How do you interact with the other inmates? If we looked at the prison through your eyes, what would we see? And he responded with a handful of sentences that in summary said, "The Karma here sucks." I laughed and shook my head. There are some questions that he's never answered and some content that he's never delivered. I assume it's his way of maintaining some semblance of freedom, to choose what it is that he says and doesn't say —and it is his memoir after all, so what does or does not get told is ultimately up to him. But that doesn't stop me from asking and asking —and asking yet again.

One day I was reading some of the half-answers he had sent and thinking that getting him to write his full story was sometimes like pulling teeth when I came across his quote about me; "She's like an oasis for me, but sometimes I get angry about her incessant questions and requests to 'go deeper'." I had a good belly laugh from that one and sent him a letter in response:

Hi Mick!
I am determined to write you a question-less letter. Can you feel me sweating from the exertion? Darnit! That was already a question!

I feel a little giddy after reading your quote about being angry at me because of my incessant probing, because your anger (and the fact that you expressed it) is so NORMAL and suggests that you are beginning to trust me to a degree —at least enough to express the tiniest bit of anger toward me. The tug-o-war that we are going through with the book's content is what almost every editor and author go through —and even more so co-authors —and it's amazing that in a very abnormal creative collaborative process-- from inside prison to outside prison and back, with mail lost and mail delays and the misunderstandings that come from not being able to hear the voice and tone and see the body language with which something was said —we have found this normalcy. I love that...

Surrounding Mickey's quote about my incessant questions were these words:

"I believe Kim and I came together through Divine intervention. She saw half my manuscript and was ready to help me with it — without ever meeting me or knowing anything about me. I have never lost faith in her or her innate harmony. I love her and her whole family."

Mickey says things like this regularly. He loves a lot of people and uses "I love you" freely and easily. I normally do too. In our household we love just about everyone and tell them so. I've even told my favorite barista at Starbucks that I love her —and I do! But with Mickey I have held back. I have been afraid to be too needed —whereas I know my Starbucks friend will never depend on me for anything more than a smile when I feel like a cup of coffee.

He has made it clear that I am his friend and am special to him. He has sent me a picture of himself. He has said things like "What would I do without you?" and "I have waited my whole life for you." What he says is *so* nice —and has completely freaked me out. His letters are full of warmth, encouragement and well wishes. He doesn't just want an editor or even a literary business partner. He wants a friend. He *needs* a friend.

The ability to stay, not fly, has entailed cultivating a new dimension to my personality. I have had to go a little deeper into my baggage and sort out what it is that has kept me perpetually on the move.

The beauty in all of this is that Mickey is not doing

anything other than being Mickey. He hasn't tried to stretch me to any new limits or do any sort of psychological makeover. He is simply sitting in his cell, day after day, writing me "hello" letters and finishing his book —a book about finding purpose in a life sentence.

The following is a sample of Mickey's early correspondence:

Dear Kim, Hello my friend. I sincerely pray this letter finds you full of light and peace. It is morning here and there is a slight wisp of fog hanging in the air—was only yesterday someone blew it up there. I am somehow renewed and my soul sighs heavily. There are a few hardy brown sparrows searching for food in no-man's land, between my window and the fence. I worry that they'll get sick from all the herbicides put out there. Nothing is able to grow there.

Ben and Eliza must have been very excited about Halloween. Seven is an age where everything is magical and I bet they couldn't wait to fill their bags with treats. What fun it must be to be their mom and be part of the magic with them.

I did not receive the fall leaves that you and the kids sent me, but the blue jay feather is taped next to one of your art prints. Thank you. My cell feels brighter with the colors and creativity.

Enclosed are my answers to your questions about the details of the riot and my feelings during that time. I hope they are satisfactory.

They will be around to pick up mail soon, so I'd better bring this one to an end.

I will close this letter, but not my heart. Give a fond hello to Jeff and the kids for me.

Mickey

The Descent

"The cell doors will remain open one hour prior to your march to the mess hall to eat meals. The tier door will be shut, but you will be allowed to mill around on the Run," said the written announcement that was taped to the tier door. It was signed by the Chief of Security. It was 1976 and hostility stemming from the '73 riot had not yet run its course. There was still no outdoor exercise permitted and hate was strong on every side.

Our cells were five feet wide and eight feet deep. The walls were ¼ -inch steel and windowless. There were windows placed on the outside Run, and if you happened to live on the third or fourth floor you could see over the prison wall, into the free world. Suffice it to say, the third and fourth Runs were the coveted Runs to live on. I lived on the first and second floors.

We were locked in our tiny cement cages for twenty-three hours a day.

The atmosphere in the prison at this time reeked of resentment, self-pity, frustration and hatred. The guards were also on edge, angry and determined to punish us for what we had done. The hatred going both directions was palpable. I had never really bothered to feel much compassion for my fellow humans and so was just as wrapped up in hatred and self-pity as the rest of the inmates. I did nothing to improve my conditions because I was convinced that I wasn't to blame for them. My unhappiness was everyone else's fault; the guards, the unjust world in which I lived, my mother because she didn't show me enough love, my father because he talked me into committing robbery. It was during this time that my listlessness became bitterness. My mind was becoming dark with paranoia and distrust. I was losing touch with long-held moral values and replacing them with the ones embraced by the twisted prison subculture.

Life was without meaning. An insect was eating away at my brain.

.

"A man who will bow down to nothing cannot bear the burden of himself." - Dostoevsky

"The lamp of the body is the eye. If therefore your eye is good, you whole body will be full of light. But if your eye is bad, your whole body will be full of darkness." - Matthew 6:22-23

I was losing my mind and my dominion over attitude was long gone. I became incensed over anything, even a minor difference. Every emotion I had ever stuffed, every injustice I had ever experienced, came flooding out in a torrent of rage with no safe channel for its outlet.

The days passed and my mind became more and more an extension of my cell. Somewhere in the previous three years a light had been snuffed out and I did not know how to release myself from the darkness. My rationality was a shallow trench that left me existing, but not quite living. I did not know how to climb out of the trench.

"Undeterred"

Silence shuffled
Out of the cell;
Crept along tiers
Cold gray
Chilling souls
Inside and out –

Broken shells
Onto Steely
Feely fears
Torn asunder

Machiavelli
Loading handguns
Blowing holes
In Nietzsche's mind

Hands behind
Blind moments
Knives punching
Cutting
Blood flowing
What I could not see
Flesh torn asunder
In the life of me

Mickey Owens

A Wrench in the Machinery

I was about fourteen and had made it into the seventh grade when I decided that I was quitting school. My mother was really upset about my decision and told me I would do no such thing, but I was too big for a whipping so she felt she had no choice but to relent. I suppose most parents would've said something like, "You will go to school or you will not live here," but it either didn't occur to her that she had that leverage, or she knew that given those options, I might opt to try it on my own. She too was epileptic and had grown up with frequent, intensely embarrassing and socially scarring seizures, so maybe her pity for me caused her to let the subject drop too easily. Maybe she already saw me as a lost cause. Whatever the case, seventh grade was when I left school.

I hated school. I was introverted and quiet. I spent much of my time alone reading. My favorite topic was Greek mythology, with all its symbolism about the human experience. I also liked to read the biographies of great Native American chiefs, like Sitting Bull, Crazy Horse and Chief Joseph of the Nez Perce Tribe. These interests bonded me with no one. I was completely un-athletic and the last one picked for the team. Even more impactful was my epilepsy. After having several seizures (although it only takes one) I was labeled a freak and called "spaz" and "retarded." Both the teacher and the students were afraid of me. Fear becomes contempt when you see some kid on the floor flopping around during class. School was a supremely uncomfortable and unhappy place for me. School was a place in which I felt badly about myself and badly about my fellow humans. They were cruel.

But my life wasn't all reclusive misery. I had some good moments too, even one having to do with sports. In elementary school I joined our baseball team, called the Columbus Zebras, sponsored by the YMCA. We played other schools in Oklahoma City. The cost to join the team was fifteen dollars and my mom grumbled about the cost, but paid it anyway. Because my mom had made the financial sacrifice for me to play ball, I felt I had to stick it out, even when it turned out that I was much more a liability than an asset to the team.

I struck out whenever I was at bat and always approached the plate trembling, knowing I would fail my team yet again. I also dropped the ball more often than not in the outfield. My teammates would groan each time it was my turn to bat. But the last game of the season, we traveled to Noble, Oklahoma and played in their ballpark. When it came my turn to bat, I stepped up to the plate and everyone looked away, knowing it was too painful to watch –until they heard the bat connect with the ball. We watched the ball sail over the heads of the outfielders. It was a homerun. When I touched home plate everyone shouted my name and slapped me on the back. I was elated and for just an instant felt the joy of being accepted.

After quitting school, I got a job mowing lawns and sold newspapers for a short, rotund man named Giuseppe. He worked for the Oklahoma City Times and had about ten boys working under him, each with their own street corner. We would be issued a bundle of sixty papers and left on our street corner until 2:00

am, selling papers to people sitting in their cars at the stop light. I received a percentage of the profits of each newspaper that I sold. It was sometimes cold, but I kept warm by dashing in and out between cars yelling, "Sunday Papers! Sunday Papers! Get 'em early!" I always sold my entire bundle of papers by the time Giuseppe came by to pick me up.

I liked working. I found my own work, did it on my own and it felt good to have no one around to label or judge me. I kept most of the money that I made, but put some toward the food and rent for our family. I liked being able to contribute, if even a little.

But even at that young age, I had a past that I was running from and feelings that I didn't want to feel. I began laying the groundwork for morphine addiction and a lifelong pattern of self-sabotage: fix, nod, steal, busted, rehab or incarceration, release, then right back to the beginning again. I had trouble allowing my life to be good. When the machinery of my life was running smoothly and well, I'd feel a little too close to the feelings that I didn't want to feel and I'd find some big wrench to throw into it.

So it was that in 1969 I was sent by the exasperated Juvenile Court to another State Training School for boys near Helena, Oklahoma. I had been caught stealing a shirt from a department store. I was placed in a cottage with other new arrivals, ages ranging from 13 to 15 years. The Rule was that before you could take a step out of your cubicle, use the restroom, watch T.V. or drink water from the fountain, permission had to be granted by a guard/supervisor. To proceed without asking would result with a smart slap to the face. Everyone failed to ask at least once. Up until that time I abhorred violence. I did not like to fight, and only did so in self-defense. I thought murder was a most terrible crime, the worse thing a man could do. But the incessant bullying and slapping by these scoundrels was beginning to paint a dim landscape in the corners of my mind.

One morning one of the youngsters left his cubicle unannounced and went to pee. The supervisor noticed and immediately headed toward the child, his palm open, wearing a shit-eating grin. But it was the last child he was to slap in that place. As he returned from the draconian drama, another youngster met him in the corridor, a Louisville Slugger in his hands. A look of fear took over the supervisor's face but was soon replaced with pain as the boy smashed the wooden bat upon his head, not once but several times. Blood and hair stained the corridor. I felt somehow vindicated. That's all I felt. I do not know what became of the man, or even if he survived. They came and carried him away in an ambulance and I never saw him again. The youngster escaped over the fence and I never saw him again either.

Life and Death in a Stinking Hole

The cell doors opened each morning, allowing people to walk up and down the Run, conversing, visiting, and so on. But I would remain in my cell, observing people as they passed.

One man peered at me in a malicious fashion each time he walked by; peering in with eyes of evil intent. I could tell he was hoping to catch me unaware so that he might pounce upon any weakness he saw in me. I knew his type – this hell hole was teeming with minds like his.

I needed to put an end to this torment. I was determined to kill this man – not for what he'd done to me, but to save myself, to grant me redemption through the blood of an evil human being.

I obtained a shank for five packs of cigarettes. It was about six inches long and razor sharp. I knew it would kill.

I sat in darkness. The night was long. I did not ponder the right or wrong of what I planned to do; only the logistics. I had never committed murder before.

I was calm. It was as if I had waited my whole life to express this feeling. Maybe I had. Oh, yes, this was the pinnacle: life and death in a stinking hole.

The morning arrived with the opening of doors, one by one. It was done manually. When the guard was finished he left the Run and closed the tier door. I waited ten minutes while I tied a strip of leather from my wrist to the handle of the shank. I stood and put my hand in my back pocket, concealing the knife. I stepped on the Run and slowly walked to his cell. I felt a jolt of consciousness and fear course through my body, and for a moment nearly called it off, but I did not and kept walking.

When I entered his cell he was standing in his boxer shorts, turned toward a shelf above his bunk. He turned to me and whispered, "No!" He saw that his death was looming.

I charged him with the knife and stabbed while he slammed against the back wall of his cell. He cried out for me to stop but I could not. Would not.

Blood was spraying everywhere in the frenzy, the blood of arteries, heart and lungs.

At one point the leather broke from my wrist and my hand slid down the bloody handle and severed one of my fingers. The knife fell to the floor but there was no point in retrieving it. Blood was everywhere and he had slipped and fallen onto his bunk. He was breathing, but with a gurgling sound. I could tell that his lungs were filling with blood. I had stabbed him thirty times and he was dying.

I sat on the floor, in the blood, and stared. I waited for him to expire. I said, "I'm sorry, I'm very sorry." I could not understand. I scooped blood from the floor and rubbed it in my eyes, thinking this insane gesture might allow me to see the same death he saw. "Please forgive me!" I cried out. And I meant it. A strong wave of remorse passed through me. But the deed was done and there was nothing I could do now to change it. He was dead. I walked away, sadness like cement blocks on my shoulders, my severed finger dangling from my hand.

There was the smell of fear as I passed the inmates on the Run. Since I was secretly very afraid of my environment, a part of me had hoped that in murdering a man, people would be afraid of me and I would be left alone. But what I felt from my fellow inmates was not a respectful fear, but a fear born out of the contempt for a psychologically sick individual. I felt more alone than I had ever felt in my life.

I stepped into my cell to clean the blood from my body. But not from my soul. I had just killed a man, and this fact would never be entirely expiated from my being or my identity.

Dear Kim,
Greetings and best wishes to you!

It is Thanksgiving and we are on lockdown due to a shortage of staff. We are usually on lockdown during holidays for this reason. This afternoon they will slide trays of food into our cells that contain the canned version of a Thanksgiving meal: Turkey, dressing, green beans, mashed potatoes and if we're lucky we'll get pumpkin pie.

Today I am thankful for you, your letters and the help you are giving me with my book. I am excited about the book and that my story might serve some useful purpose.

May this day find you surrounded by the love of family and aware of the great blessings that are around and within you. Give a hello to Eliza (the aspiring artist!) and Ben (the budding inventor!) from me and to Jeff too.

Mickey

Hi Mickey,

I am so glad that you found something to feel thankful about on Thanksgiving. I wondered if, having been in prison for almost forty years, you still feel any connection to the holiday or its traditions —or any connection to feeling particularly thankful for that matter. With your crazy upbringing, I wonder if you even had Thanksgivings as a child —did you? What were they like?

Does being in prison for decades hone one's ability to be thankful, to find things to be grateful for in unexpected places, or does the need to numb your mind to surroundings in order to not feel constantly short-changed also numb your ability to swing the other direction into gratitude?

I live what most would consider a blessed and lucky life and yet there are still days when I don't feel thankful at all. There are days when I feel sorry for myself, in my nice house, my free, prosperous country, with my sweet husband and two healthy, bright, kind children. Sometimes I wonder if I'm thankfulness disabled.

Getting letters from you almost every day and reading through your story, I cannot help but see how ridiculous and self-indulgent my lack of gratitude is. I see my life through your eyes and am consistently reminded not to take my many blessings for granted.

I am thank-full for you and for our collaboration and for the way you unwittingly remind me to notice the good in my life. But most of all, I am thankful for this connection that we have and the work that we are doing because for the first time in my life, I am no longer restless and focusing on some distant future in which I will be happier and more fulfilled. I am no longer climbing a mountain simply for the sake of getting somewhere other than where I am. I am content, Mickey, and I don't believe I have ever experienced contentment before. It is this work that we are doing that has both anchored me so that I am no longer adrift and provided me with a purpose for which I feel joy. I am grateful for this work and for our friendship. Love, Kim

God Seeped In

I had killed a man. I did not know how I could live with that. Following a shakedown, they removed me from General population and placed me in a death cell, underground, near the electric chair. These cells were normally used to house a death-row inmate 24 hours prior to execution.

There were no lights or electrical outlets; the only dim illumination was cast by lights outside the cells. Steel wire mesh covered the doors, with an opening toward the bottom that facilitated the passing of food trays in and out.

Once a day I was allowed one hour of exercise in a large room that was normally used for witnesses of an execution. Noticing the electric chair, I had a vision of sitting in it, the electricity coursing through my brain and body until I was dead. I understood the consequences of what I had done.

I spent six weeks there and then was moved up to Administrative Segregation on ground level.

In Ad-Seg I was placed in a single cell, 5 x 8 feet. This tier was a lock-up unit that held cons suspected of a wide variety of crimes, from homicide to drug dealing to escape attempts. It was a jail within a prison. Some had been languishing there for two or three years, waiting for what they hoped would be vindication. They would be in for a long wait.

I didn't think there was a deeper hell than living with having killed a man. I was wrong. Living with having killed a man in Ad-Seg, with nothing to do but relive what I had done not only kept the wound open, but let it fester. I spent a year on Ad-Seg and was not allowed to mix with the other prisoners nor any time outdoors. I descended a little deeper into darkness every day.

I grew tired of having no one to talk to. Some days I did not come out of my cell for my fifteen minutes alone in the hall, preferring the narrow confines of my cell like a mother's womb. It was *my* cell. It talked to me, told me of its former occupants, when men were beaten with whips and carried a ball and chain. I felt their hatred and their sorrow and empathized; I loved them, I knew the cell spoke to them, too, and there were many stories, told and untold, which echoed against the steel walls.

I knew their bodies were buried in the inmate graveyard long, long ago – but their stories remained, and I heard them: the one who bashed in his mother's head with a frying pan because she failed to make him pancakes for breakfast but asked God for forgiveness and thought he was saved. And there was the old man who killed a fellow over the price of a watermelon and someone called the sheriff. He got life and they made him walk to the prison with a rope tied to a buggy.

I stopped eating and lost 30 pounds. I attempted suicide twice – cut my arms and wrists but they sewed them back together and returned me to my cell. I suffered guilt for what I had done and felt shame. The cell told me that I would never leave and that my life was effectively over. The time came when nothing except death had meaning. I was deeply bedeviled and completely broken. There were cracks in my armor; I had nothing left to defend or fight for. My ego was rubble; I had no concept of who I was or my place in the world, and there was no foundation on which to rebuild. The complete absence of hope, or love, or even the comfort of a human touch left gaping holes in my psyche. I was all cracks and holes and rubble. I was broken open. God seeped in. I welcomed Him.

As soon as I opened myself to God, light began seeping in too. There was a guy named Truman who was serving a life sentence and he was allowed time out of his cell once per day to sweep and mop the Run. Because he passed each cell while he worked, he was able to keep tabs on what was going on with the inmates. Apparently he had noticed how much pain I was in, because he stopped at my cell and said, "You know, Mickey, you can't escape your karma through suicide." He then handed me a little alka-seltzer packet and walked away. It contained a small amount of marijuana. I immediately rolled a joint. It was powerful. I lay back on my bunk and relaxed, silently grateful for his generous gift, and for the brief escape. I wondered at his words, and although I did not completely understand them, I felt truth in them. I knew suicide was not the answer – but then what was?

Over the months that followed, Spirit began moving in my soul, performing its healing, while Truman loaned me books on all forms of spirituality, everything from the Bhagavid Gita to the Holy Scriptures. He loaned me a book called *Be Here Now*, which taught self-forgiveness. Truman and I once talked about religion versus mental illness. He pointed to an air vent in the wall and said, "If you wrote the warden and told him that you are unmistakably hearing God's voice speak to you through that vent, he would notify the prison psychiatrist to keep an eye on you. If you wrote the chaplain and related the same thing, he would say that God works in mysterious ways. Fact is, in either case, you are hearing what nobody else is." We both laughed and it felt so good to laugh. It felt good to talk and learn and open my eyes to that which cannot be seen. I learned how to meditate and practiced each day. Slowly, my mind pieced itself together, but in a new configuration.

A word on forgiveness: If a man forgives himself, he can forgive anyone. It is not a condoning of what has been done. It is a letting go of the past and embracing the present. There is no point in repeatedly scratching an old wound until it bleeds.

Truman was likely one of the most intelligent people I have ever met. We had talks that left me with thoughts light as a feather, thoughts I later shared with other troubled young cons. At this point I would be remiss not to mention two other angels that were sent to me during this time.

Truman told me about Bo and Sita Lozoff, of the Prison Human Kindness Project. They sent me books and literature filled with love and positive self-discovery. I began writing them letters, mostly just to have someone to "talk" to, but sometimes to ask questions as well. I wrote them regularly for about seven years. Some of my letters were friendly and positive, while many were paranoid and disturbed.

They published a book called; *We're All Doing Time*, in which some of these letters –the good and the ugly -- appear. In fact, in these letters is captured one of the most difficult periods and perhaps the lowest psychological points of my life. The letters published in Bo's book come from a time in which I not only felt paranoid and suicidal, but in which I consciously experienced my first true anger. Even when I murdered my fellow inmate, my attack was not (consciously at least) fueled by anger, but by paranoia, despondency and a demented symbolism – I was attempting to destroy the "monster," not fully grasping that the monster was not this other man, but something that lived in me.

I had been in administrative segregation for over a year when a new guy was assigned the cell next to mine. His name was Paul and I discovered that he, like me, was disillusioned with the surface of things, searching but never finding. His eyes were wide open. I began sending "kites" (letters) to him with instructions on meditation and how to perform Asanas (Hatha Yoga) and loaned him my spiritual books. Paul was like a sponge. He absorbed everything I sent him with vigor. He immediately took to Bo and Sita's philosophies and soon began writing them letters. Paul and I had long, deep conversations while still in our cells and became close friends before we had even seen each other's faces. When we were released from Ad-Seg and free to go out in the yard, he and I would spend hours there discussing mostly Zen Buddhism. We were growing at the same time and provided each other with a lot of support through this growth. Later in our friendship, when I would lose myself in fear and darkness, it was his light that would often dispel the delusions. We were cellies for many years and I do not believe I would have made it through without him. Other times, when I was well, it was I who offered him advice. He was the best friend I'd ever had.

I went to trial in 1977 and was found guilty of second degree manslaughter after only a few hours of deliberation. The following month, the judge sentenced me to an indeterminate term of ten years to life, to run consecutively to the two years and the 25 years that I was already serving. I was 22 years old. I did not believe I would ever see the free world again. This consequence was a wake-up call that shifted my perception; a turning point and a defining moment, ending forever an old way of thought.

Thanks to Truman, Bo and Sita and the many books I had read, I had grown to see the unity between myself and the world in which I lived. Somewhere from within came the urge to bring peace to the internal and external warring in my life, the internal and external insanity. Somewhere in the midst of my life sentence, came a life purpose.

We convicts tend to believe that life has nothing to offer us, but through my correspondence with Bo and Sita and the books that I read, I learned to ask myself what it was that I was offering to life. I realized that life gives us as much happiness as we put into it.

I also came to really believe that our Creator loves us all and that we are all eligible for His blessings and grace. When we knock, He truly does answer. With this in mind, I knew I had to become involved. Somewhere within me I found a courage that I hadn't previously known I possessed.

Kim

I was curious about Mickey's letters to Bo and Sita. I wondered about the man he was back then and how he expressed himself. I wanted to better know that part of Mickey. I wanted to know what other people's impressions were of Mickey. I ordered the book (We're All Doing Time) in which Mickey's letters are published. I did this partly because our friendship was blossoming and as is typical of new friendships, I wanted get to know my friend better. Not being able to experience him in person, or even hear his voice and the nuances in a voice that tell one so much about a person, I wanted to hear from some people who had experienced him firsthand.

I also ordered the book because I was still very skittish when it came to Mickey. I found myself apprehensive every time I'd get a letter from him, wondering if he'd express something about himself that would scare me, or if I might have asked or written something that had angered him or scared him away. I wanted to know that I could safely have a friendship with him. Because he so closely matched the personality profile of men I had dated, I waited for him to explode and lose control, just as they had. I wanted Mickey's letters to show that when he lost his mind and committed murder, it had been his breaking point, a time in which he unleashed a lifetime worth of pain and that since that time he had been relatively stable. That wasn't the case.

When the book arrived on my doorstep, I opened the package with both intense curiosity and dread. Despite the fact that the book is 317 pages, I opened it straight to Mickey's letters. I also discovered many letters from his friend Paul that gave glimpses, both into Mickey and into the depth of their friendship.

Mickey had been very open in his description of the emotional and psychological state that he was in while committing murder and the even deeper descent he experienced afterward, but I was still shell-shocked by the venom and paranoia in some of his letters. I nicknamed them the "F-you letters." What was even more striking was that these letters were written, not during the post-murder period, but several years later. He'd had at least one other very deep psychological descent –a dark and angry period that lasted a long time. This really scared me. Why hadn't he told me about that? Had he gone crazy other times? Could writing this book and the harsh memories send him in a downward spiral? Might I do something that would accidentally set off the tripwire to another emotional explosion? Were we walking through a minefield? I wondered what else he hadn't told me. I felt stirred up and a little sick to my stomach. My trust in him was shaken.

Mickey felt my distrust. He felt me distance myself. His trust in *me* was shaken. I was another person who was abandoning him. I got my very own "F-you" letter -- only without any "F-bombs." His anger was defensive; *"I am not a faggot and I am not a liar!"* and entailed the construction of an armor with which to protect himself from the unveiling of facts for which (I later learned) he felt ashamed, *"You are turning this into something for the Jerry Springer Show, so it's your book. Say whatever you want about me and sell it to Oprah. I don't want anything to do with*

My heart hurt for having caused him pain and for putting him in a place where he felt the need to defend himself. He, in turn, felt terrible for being angry. He kept apologizing, letter after letter. I could also tell that letter-writing had left too much room for misunderstandings. He thought that I was upset about things that I was not upset about. I felt terrible because he continued to feel terrible. We were a hot mess. But things always get messier when you're getting them cleaned up. All the junk has to come out of the shed in order to figure out what's still of use and what's garbage. It was a lengthy upheaval with the communication being done through letters, but afterward we were in a better place than we had been before. We had both passed each other's tests –I didn't abandon him even when he got angry and he didn't go off the psychological deep end when things got rough.

Once the dust had settled—once both our fears had been quelled -- I could understand why Mickey hadn't wanted to unbury that part of his life, especially for all to see. It had not only been an excruciatingly painful time for him, but I imagine that Mickey feels weak and more of a failure (as if being in prison for life isn't enough) to have gone so low a second time. I think that, more than anything, he is ashamed of the anger he expresses in his letters. I gather from what he has told me of his life (and what his friend Paul says about Mickey in his letters) that Mickey is not comfortable expressing anger. Like many of us, he believes he is only loveable if he is kind. He's the type of person who gives everything he can, both materially and energetically, in order to earn people's love. He's told me that even at the age of 56, he still works on feeling loveable and of value, not for what he can offer others, but for who he is.

Mickey has spent his whole life skating on the thin ice of acceptability. Being epileptic, un-athletic, lower class, too smart, introverted, the child of drug-addicted and incarcerated teenage parents and a world class screw-up from an early age, he's had to work extra hard at being acceptable. Anger is the one emotion I'm sure Mickey felt would knock him out of the acceptability ring. This being the case, he's held his anger in an emotional reservoir for years upon years. The thing about emotional reservoirs is that they ultimately get full and burst —and NO ONE wants to be around when that happens, especially the person it's happening to.

I'm like Mickey in this way and am the last one who should judge him for his rage. When my own reservoir has been tapped, I've been known to come at people like a bitch on a bulldozer. It is only through Divine intervention that I have friends, family and a husband who still love me.

I would love for Mickey's story to be a "made for Hollywood" recipe, in which he goes through one extraordinarily challenging time, transcends it and then goes into his happy ending. But the fact is that Mickey's journey —as is the case for all of us -- has highs and lows and middle areas that come in no predictable pattern. How we are doing in any given moment depends on what life has most recently served us and which emotional circuits have been triggered by those events.

Bo says it perfectly when he describes Mickey's letters:

> "It's not a simple, clear cut story like 'I was blind, but now I see, thanks a lot.' It's more the way life really is for most of us; 'I was blind. I saw again. I was blind again, I saw again…' This correspondence is also a good reminder not to close the books prematurely on any of us or on our friends, because change often seems to strike as unpredictably as lightning."

Dear Friends,

I am a prisoner here at OSP, where I am presently incarcerated on a lock-up unit known as "administrative segregation." I am not allowed yard privileges, and am only allowed out of my cell for approximately one hour a day.

A couple of weeks ago, a friend let me borrow an issue of INSIDE-OUT. Now that I have read it a good many times (and will continue), I can only say that what I saw before as a hopeless situation has now become a blessing to my spiritual growth.

Indeed, instead of spending all of this idle time feeling sorry for myself, I now use it in positive ways. I have a full day and night (with only minor interruptions) to devote to meditation and hatha yoga. It's a perfect setting for doing asanas (postures). I have begun to really dig this beautiful solitude, believe me!

I wish to thank you for the good work you are currently doing and sincerely hope that you will continue.

In spiritual love,
Mickey/Oklahoma

[six months later]

Dear Friends,
Sincerely hope this finds all of the family there in good health and good spirits! I received the holiday card and have it pasted on the wall. It helps a great deal in my meditations.

I doubt that you would remember my last letter to you since it was several months ago and I'm sure you must get a large amount of mail from other prisoners daily. In my last letter I said that I was at that time in administrative segregation where I was awaiting trial for stabbing and killing another inmate, 18 months previously.

Last September I was finally tried and received a sentence of 10 years to life —to be served after the completion of my current sentence of 28 years.

To say that I wasn't shaken by it would be untrue. I was in fact shaken a great deal, with a month or two of self-pity to ice the cake. But I know where that's at by now. Nothing can be changed one iota through indulgences of the lower self. Grist for the mill, every bit of it. I am in a perfect position to clean up my karma and work on myself and intend to continue doing so.

So here we are now, as Ram Dass says. It's ours to do what we want with it. Love, that's the key, I'm sure.

Please keep up the wonderful work. Hope to be seeing the next newsletter soon.

God bless you, I send love and peace,

Mickey

Black and White

I was twelve years old and had been caught with marijuana. The court sent me to the Oklahoma State Training School in Boley, Oklahoma. Even at that young age, the only time I ever felt happy was when I was high on something. So many people in my family were addicted to drugs that many times I would find myself sitting alone in the living room while everyone else was in the bathroom getting high. I think part of my attraction to drugs was simply that I wanted to be where everyone else was. But drugs and alcohol also took me out of a loneliness and sadness that I couldn't seem to otherwise rise above.

It could be that the brains of my family were hardwired so that we needed a chemical boost to experience what other people experienced as normal. Maybe we were all just depressed and self-medicating. It's hard to say whether the depression in my family was more circumstantial or biological, because depression is such a vicious cycle. When depressed, it's hard to find the motivation to make a happy life and the bleak lives we settle for are breeding grounds for deeper depression. In any case, I was step-for-step in line with the family tradition of chemical addiction, underachievement and trouble with the law.

Boley was a black town and the population in the Reform School was 90% black. The staff was entirely black. They had recently integrated the State institutions and I was one of the first whites to go there. Martin Luther King had very recently been assassinated, so anger toward white people was especially strong. Some of the inmates were abusive and violent toward me because of my color. I'm sure they looked at me and saw a stupid white boy, a racist--and to their credit, that's exactly what I was.

I was eventually accepted by the blacks at the school because I didn't ever react with anger. Some even accepted me as a friend. The black kids at Boley were the same as me, just a different color. We all hurt, feared, laughed and lived the same.

I worked in the dairy for a while, milking cows. Later I was assigned a job in the chicken coop gathering eggs. One other black youngster was assigned with me. His name was Frankie and after gathering and washing the eggs, we would take empty wooden crates, line them up next to the furnace and sleep until dawn. He told me he had no parents, that both had died of cancer. At the time, both of mine still lived and while they were nobody's idea of ideal parents, I couldn't fathom going through life without them. I sympathized greatly and we became the best of friends. We were like brothers.

I believe I was put in that mostly black school for a higher reason. I had been a racist before getting to know and understand people of color. Although I was at the school only a short time, the respect I learned to feel for people of all colors and stripes was a strong foundation for a more purposeful and contributing role for the rest of my life.

The Test

A few months passed and one morning the lieutenant came to my cell and told me I was being placed back into the General Population. I had been in lockdown and hadn't seen the light of day for eighteen months.

The inmate I killed didn't have many friends, but some, and it was these men whom I would have to confront. I wanted to do so peaceably, but there was nothing to guarantee that this would be the case. They could have been arming themselves at that moment, preparing for an act of revenge to honor their friend. I understood.

Prior to going out to the yard I stuffed thick magazines into my trousers that partly covered my sides and torso, in case I was stabbed. I obtained a shank and stuck it in my sock. His homeys had been pointed out to me by a friend. When I came out to the yard, there were three of his friends there, gathered beneath one of the guard towers. If their intention was to kill me, they would be successful. One I might handle. Three I could not. I approached with some anxiety. I introduced myself and explained that I felt bad about what I had done and that if I could cross the edge and bring him back with me, I would. I asked for forgiveness. And forgiveness is what I received. Each of them said it was cool, but did not shake my offered hand and asked that I keep a distance for now. I nodded and thanked them and turned away. Nothing more happened and I breathed a sigh of relief. It was time to move on and to do so with purpose.

The first test of my commitment to peacemaking came when I was transferred to Granite Prison, so called because its backyard contained a quarry. There was a great deal of animosity between the Whites and African-Americans at Granite. It was summertime and the sticky heat made for short tempers and quick resentments. Tensions were strong.

Things came to a head on a hot summer day when a black accused a white of stealing sun shades from him. The black, who went by the name of Cinque, demanded that the white, whose name was Brian, either return his property or face grave consequences. Already, blacks and whites were squaring off in the yard, some armed with shanks and clubs. I did not want to see more insanity. I did some quick investigation and discovered that Cinque's cell partner had stolen the glasses and told two blacks that he sold them to a "white boy" for cocaine. That white boy was Brian. The culprit then went into protective custody.

The guards in the towers had noticed the gathering and had ventured out on the tower walkways, armed with mini-14's, ready to cut down on the rabble if they became troublesome.

On the yard, taunts and insults were being exchanged by both races. Despite this, I made my way to Cinque and told him what had really happened. One angry black beside him said, "Yeah, then why didn't he give 'em back, white boy?" I answered that he did not know they had been stolen. I told him that I would talk to Brian and propose that they talk about it, one-on-one, before any violence ensued. "And what are you gonna do to stop us?" another inmate asked. "Well," I answered, "maybe nothing. But what I see is the blacks on one side and the whites on the other and it just shouldn't be that way. This shit really ain't about nothing." I then proceeded over to Brian and he agreed to speak civilly to Cinque. They came together and it was agreed that Cinque would reimburse Brian the money he spent if he could get his shades back. Brian agreed. The crowd slowly dispersed with many on both sides still angry. They had been cheated out of blood lust, for which they had psyched themselves up. But no one would lose a loved one that day --and in that hot prison yard, I had done something purposeful.

Love and Loss

In the Spring of 1978 a good friend of mine who had been released a year before returned to prison for killing his wife's father. He came with a new sentence of thirty years. His name was Mickey, same as mine.

He was still very much in love with his wife. It appeared that she was an indirect cause of what landed him back inside.

Her father had a penchant for beating his daughter whenever he was distressed. In Mickey's world the solution was a violent one.

Following a visit to her parent's house his wife returned home with a cut lip and a black eye. It was the last straw for Mickey. He became enraged, found a gun and went to see her father. He shot and killed him on the spot.

Following Mickey's conviction she moved to the prison town of McAlester, so that she would be closer to him. Mickey was elated that she was so near.

He was serving a long sentence and rarely does a young couple remain married for that lengthy a prison sentence. They were apart in every way. I had witnessed more heart wrenching divorces in prison than I cared to count. But love is strong and every man wants to believe his wife will remain faithful. I prayed this would be the case for my friend. I hoped for a miracle.

None was forthcoming.

A guard who lived in McAlester told Mickey that his wife was rumored to be living with another man. Mickey went to the line of inmate telephones and dialed his wife's number. A man answered. He hung up the receiver slowly and turned away.

"You know, bro," I said, with a hand on his shoulder, "whatever it is it will look better tomorrow, even if it doesn't feel that way now."

"Yeah, yeah, I know," he said. I'll talk to you it later." He shuffled off. Later that night he hung himself.

> When I died
> I thought I heard
> In somber voice intone;
> "Rest in peace
> O weary soul,"
> But why should I
> have to ask
> Upon reflection
> Of the light,
> Need the blessing
> For the waking
> Not the ending
> Of my life.
> Mickey Owens

Mom

My mother remained my helper and friend throughout the years of 1973 to 1979. She came to see me most visiting days (visits were allowed once a month) to reassure me that I was not alone and that I was still cared for. We were allowed to sit at a small circular table together. She was in her early forties and still looked beautiful. She was what drug and alcohol counselors call a "functioning addict," using in moderation, but never totally free of the addiction.

Mom and I talked about God and how much better she felt about herself when I would write her letters about spirituality. She brought me love and peace when she visited. She was one of the very few bright spots in my life and I looked forward to her visits more than just about anything else.

One morning I was called to the Chaplain's Office. In the office was a priest in black with a white collar. He announced in a businesslike tone that my mother had died the day before. She had been proclaimed dead of an overdose on arrival at Community hospital in Oklahoma City.

She was only forty-two years old, but she had been a mother since sixteen and addicted to drugs since about the same age. Her life had been hard and full and I think she had been ready to die. She had assumed the drugs would kill her one day. She was resigned when it came to her addictions. There was no fight left in her and she had looked at her addictions like a last cigarette before going in front of the firing squad.

While both parents are my genetic link to addiction, my mother is my genetic link to epilepsy. Sometimes I wonder if the chemical makeup of an epileptic brain predisposes us to addiction or somehow strengthens a chemical's hold on us. What I know for sure is that both my mother and I have shared the same lack of fight when it came to our addictions. My mother saw going chemical-free as a mountain that was too hard to climb and so she rarely even bothered to take the first step. For most of my life I have felt the same way. Today, even anchored in God, I would be lured to the rocks by the siren song of drugs.

My mom was a complicated woman, a mixed bag of emotions and issues, but still so easy to love. She was not entirely sane. Insanity does run in my family. She was quiet and contemplative, yet prone to outbursts of anger. She was motherly and loving when she was high, but distant and withdrawn when not.

As a child, her alcoholic father abused her. Because she was very beautiful, she was the victim of men's lust and always felt both needy and vulnerable. Her love for my sister and I was ever-present and palpable, but she was a child herself when she began motherhood and she felt burdened and overwhelmed by us. She was relieved when we grew old enough to strike out on our own.

She died as she had lived. Quietly. As if not to bother anyone.

The chaplain who reported my mother's death said that I would be allowed to attend the graveside funeral upon receipt of $100 to pay for the escorting guard's time. I didn't have $100. I asked if he would say a prayer for her and he consented.

An uncle later contacted me and offered to pay the $100 so that I could attend the funeral. It was a large funeral because she had many friends. They were all substance abusers of one kind or another, but like my mom, they were really good people with big emotional wounds. I read a long eulogy that I had written and closed it with excerpts from her favorite book, *The Prophet*, by Khalil Gibran.

My mom was not only my best friend and supporter, but my only strong connection to the outside world. I did not know how to cope with the void that she left behind. Her passing was a tipping point for me, the straw that broke the camel's back, the last drop of emotion I could contain. The feelings that I had been holding in year after year came rushing out in a torrent and swept me down to a very deep, dark and angry place —and to another psychiatric hospital. But at that time, I simply went back to my cell, got drunk on pruno, and wept.

Kim

The death of Mickey's mom initiated for him another plunge into psychological hell.

In Bo Lozoff's book, *We're All Doing Time*, Bo says that for a few years before the death of Mickey's mom, Mickey did really well and used his prison time as if he were a monk in a cell. Around the time that Mickey's mom died, Mickey's best friend Paul also began writing letters to Bo and asked that Bo and Sita come out to do one of their programs in the prison. This they did. It was the first program allowed in the prison since the riot had occurred several years prior.

From Paul's letters and Bo's impression of Mickey when they met in person, I got a much deeper glimpse into Mickey and his state of mind at this time. It is in this chapter of Mickey's life that he wrote what I nicknamed the "F-You" letters.

The following is Bo's description, from We're All Doing Time, of the workshop and of Mickey during the workshop:

"With a total of about 50 men coming together in the hot, stifling gym, we could hardly hear each other because of the bad acoustics and the fans (no windows). But the workshop was great and it was wonderful to finally meet Paul and Mickey in person. Paul exchanged huge hugs with us, but Mickey

seemed strangely uncomfortable. I noticed that during the meditation periods, especially the eye-to-eye meditation with another inmate, he had as hard a time as any of the newcomers and he avoided eye contact with me and Sita when we spoke with him afterward.

A few months later we received the following letter from Paul about what Mickey was going through:"

Dear Bo and Sita,
For quite a few days I've debated over how and when to tell you of Mickey's current predicament. Today seems to be the day. Early last week Mickey cut himself across the neck with a razorblade in what appeared to be a suicide attempt. However, the wound wasn't too bad and physically he's safe and secure. Mentally, Mickey is in bad shape. I really don't think he was truly wanting to die, because I think he really would have if he intended to —Mickey KNOWs how to waste himself…

…I thought he was really doing good, but I knew he was having his "down days" more frequently. I just don't have the chance to be with him very much (only at mealtimes) otherwise maybe I could have helped prevent this. At any rate, I'm deeply concerned with his present state and am praying for him. I've tried to get them to let me go out to the infirmary to see him, but I don't guess they're gonna let me do that.

I saw Charlotte [Charlotte was a staff member at the prison who was kind to the inmates] *and she promised she'd check into the situation and put all her energy into helping Mickey. But I saw her again this morning and she was teary-eyed as she informed me that it looks really bad. She said he is on a severe paranoid trip and thinks nobody cares; that he doesn't have any friends in here. If only dear Mickey knew the love I have for him, he'd know he had a real friend. But like Charlotte says, he's just in that frame of mind —he's very confused. And also, he stated that he just doesn't have any energy anymore...*

...Emotionally I went way down when I heard about Mickey's state, yet spiritually I know that fuel has been added to the fire.' I'm just kinda directing all the Grace that God gives me toward Mickey right now. How can I best serve him?...
I love you both so much,
Peace and Love, Paul

(a letter Bo sent to Mickey after hearing about his struggles)

Dear Mickey,
Just a short note to say "hi" and let you know we've heard your latest news. We send all our love and blessings. We've been in touch with Paul who loves you very deeply as a brother. He tried to get in to see you last week, but they wouldn't let him.
What else can I say when I have no idea where you're at right now? I don't need to lay any trips on you, bro, just to say we're here and we love you. Drop us a line if you feel like it.

Much Love, Bo

(A portion of a letter from Paul)

Dear Bo,

Charlotte told me that Mickey received your letter. Although he was suspicious at first, he finally showed some light and told her to tell you all, "I'm not totally lost..." He's been transferred to a prison mental health center in another city...
I think the statement he made for you is a sign he's still **here***...*
Paul

(A letter from Mickey)

Dear Bo and Sita,
I sincerely hope this finds you in beautiful spirits. I received your Christmas card and the beautiful truth that St. Paul so grandly expressed. How easy it is to become engrossed in our spiritual evolvement that we lose sight of the very force that gives any of it meaning —the simple act of loving. Without it, it's all dry and empty. Yet try to grab hold and call it "mine" and it loses its magic. Love does what it will and lets it go at that...May we all grow in love and its blessing.

Bo, everything's all right. I chose to be crazy for a while but I'm back to being normal, or whatever it's called, again. I got real depressed and angry and paranoid...because I wanted to say "fuck it, that's it, I ain't dealing with this anymore. It's all got to end. It's all so stupid and empty anyway." ...and so I said it. Now I can get back to the journey. Love. You said it. The comforter Christ sent us. With it the journey's not too heavy at all.

This place where I am now is really interesting. IMHU it's called. There are eighty men here, all of whom are into some state of psychosis. They're really neat. Some of 'em are very high but they're afraid to come back down into the grossness of physical reality. Others merely choose to check out 'cause they don't like the rules. Whatever. I don't judge any of them their choices.

I am in a "group" with five other guys who have attempted suicide. I really enjoy it. I love these guys. Some are very tormented from attachments they've formed with the "free world" and have tried suicide rather than give up the attachment. But they still don't really want to die, they're just wanting to make a statement, a rebellious cry for help. I can relate to them. I try to share some of my own experiences in prison. If one of us opens up, the rest will too. I don't try to "tell" anyone how to do their time, but if I can help in the least way, it helps me in the highest way. It's good to feel free. It's good to be aware.

Christ is the Light that dispels the darkness…He said that "Where I am you may be also." It's nearly Christmas, the time of year that we celebrate that Light within where He is. May the joy of this Light shine throughout each of us and may we know that peace which is total.
I wish you both a merry Christmas.
Thanks for being who you are

I love you,
Mickey

(comments from Bo)

We had some brief correspondence with both Mickey and Paul. Mickey got transferred back to maximum and he and Paul became best friends once again....but then Paul was transferred to another prison. Just a few days before his transfer, we received the following letters from Paul and Mickey, one day apart. Mickey's came first:

Dear Bo and Sita,
Discontinue sending me your newsletter. Also your perfumed cards. I don't want to hear anymore from you people. Waste your precious endeavor on your "brother" and his monumental crusade against "sickness." You look for something to be a certain way and that's what you'll see. But like that fellow holed up in that trailer, it's either real or it ain't. I don't really give a shit one way or another. I'm tired of playing this stupid game. Don't write me anymore.
Mickey

Dear Bo and Sita,
Much love to the two of you. Bo, your comment about Mickey ("his path up the mountain") probably saved me from hurting him more than he is, or from hurting myself—as I've come to see that it is impossible to "pin" Mickey or anyone else down at all

and to even attempt in the slightest way breeds pain and suffering. Even now I haven't let go completely. I'm caught. On one side, I'm afraid that to let Mickey go would be a disaster for him, as I'm the only one in here who tries to help him. Just last week I talked him out of suicide. Yet on the other hand, Mickey swings from high to low so rapidly anymore that it seems he would be better off if I let him work it out for himself…

Just yesterday I met a very arrogant, aggressive and dangerous Mickey. This was a new personality, as before he was either totally high and happy or depressed, withdrawn and suicidal. He came to scare me yesterday. He talked of a desire to catch anyone messing him around in any way, for he claimed he wanted an excuse to hurt someone. He told me that he's not been sick at all, that he's just been playing games and for me to forget about trying to get him help.

Bo, his posture was totally different, his gestures were different, his expressions, tone of voice, energy, everything was different. This was not Mickey at all. He even managed to spook me a little.

*He told me he wrote you and told you never to write him again. Believe me, if he did, it wasn't **him** that did it, do you understand? He said the teachings are all bullshit and he got rid of all his books. Well I have no choice now, I guess…it looks like I HAVE to let go. But I can see a pattern and he'll be high again soon and wanting to help.*

I love Mickey but I don't know what to do unless it's "nothing." I'm confused, but something says, "Just play it by ear and learn to interact with his different personalities just as if he is completely different people each time." One thing, I think it would be best if you don't mention my name to him if you do write him. He gets paranoid and thinks the people who love him are plotting to hurt him.

I love you, may peace be yours,

Love, Paul

(letter from Bo to Mickey in response to their letters)

Dear Mickey,

Well you said not to write you anymore, but my mama always told me to reply to a personal letter from a friend. And whether you like it or not, you're a friend of mine. If you never write me again, you'll just be a friend who never wrote me again.

By the way, we've never owned any "perfumed cards." We're just doing our thing like you're doing yours. We may well be full of shit, but at least we're sincerely full of shit. So what are you so pissed off about?

Listen, I hope you decide to keep in touch, even just to argue. We've exchanged a lot of love and insights through the years and to me the bummers are at least as good as the "love and light" ones. Do you think that Sita and I never get depressed or cynical?...

Try opening to the pain and fear instead of shutting it out or allowing it to take you over. You can do it. I've been there and I know how cold and scary it can get…You can make it Mick; it may take all the effort you've got and all that you can pray for, but you can do it…meanwhile, Sita and I still love you dearly and we hope you don't chalk us up. We don't need to save your soul, just say "hi" every now and then.

Love,

Bo

(nearly a year later)

Dear Bo and Sita,

I sincerely hope this letter finds you and your son well and in good spirits. I received your letter a few months ago. Thank you for writing in response to the letter I wrote you, in which I said not to write me anymore. I appreciate the fact that you did anyway.

I am still your friend, of course. I suppose I always will be. It was your message which, in 1975, stirred an awakening in me that probably saved my life, though that is not such a big deal. What is such a big deal is the understanding that came with it and is still coming as I grow older…

Your message is essentially the same as it's always been. But it's cloaked in a different form now. For a while it was centered on the "higher Self" or that "one Within." Now it's mainly concerned with how to cut through suffering and pain. I realize you're not into "how-to" lessons, so maybe I expressed that wrong. But then you can't tell anyone how to get out of their suffering any more than a rock can become a fish. All you can do is tell 'em most people don't give a fuck whether they're suffering or not, because they're too caught in their own private hells and so they'd best find their own way out.

Yes, I'm sure it would be a good response to say, "Maybe I can't tell them the way out, but I can love them" as if that means anything.

Love. What does it mean? Ram Dass tells us it ain't attachment. St. Paul tells us it's unconditional. But I've never known love that wasn't based on some form of gratification or attachment.

…I've never met a single being who did not enjoy hearing the words "I love you" but I've never met one either who did not enjoy hearing how great a person they were. Where is the detachment, the unconditionality in this?

The love you speak of is beyond my understanding. And the other love, the attachment stuff, is probably the cause of more pain than anything I ever knew. And you call this "Life." I understand why so many people are afraid to live. Or to "love?"

Now you want to tell me that if we don't "get it right" this lifetime, we'll just have to do it all over again. How do you know? What makes you so convinced anybody'll have to do anything again? I've read all the metaphysical stuff on natural laws and what-not, and most of 'em are no more than assumptions. It all comes down to the age-old admonishment of punishment, or the offer of reward, if you think a certain way.

Even a white rat in a cage learns to play that game after a while. Or fear it. It's just one more brainwashing technique.

Fear. Let's talk about fear, my friends. Not necessarily fear of bodily harm, but fear of being degraded and humiliated in a world where such things are much more harmful to your chances of getting by than anything else.

Beginning the year before and continuing up until the late summer of last year, it became increasingly hard to deal with my environment. Long-time "friends" took it upon themselves to play games with my mind. If you've been in touch with Paul then you probably already know what I'm talking about. If you don't, well, it really doesn't need an explanation. You weren't there. You didn't breathe that shit being sprayed into my cell night after night. You didn't stink of it, while everyone was laughing. You didn't see the pretense. Even my own sister and brother on the streets played the little game. But they didn't ingest the shit that damaged my liver and intestinal tract permanently, as I discovered at Easter State Hospital last summer. Nor are they taking seizure medication for a fucked-up brain that resulted from all this shit.

Yeah, I must be paranoid schizophrenic. And maybe my actions fit that label, but what happened wasn't my imagination or a hallucination. And the results goddamn sure weren't.

Now I don't know whether or not you people were, in your own way, playing a game with me or not. And I don't care if you were. I don't believe that you would ever intentionally hurt anyone, especially someone whom you've cared about for so long a time as me. But then, who knows? I no longer try to understand what motivates people. Whenever someone in here would express their pain and I would try to help with words that I thought may enlighten, they would only become further distant and ridicule me for acting like some great teacher. Their ridicule turned to spite pretty quickly. So fuck them. At the present time I am doing 60 days on the disciplinary unit for assaulting an officer and "disrespecting" him. I didn't have any motive for doing it. I was just drunk and angry. And a little paranoid. You see, brother, when you ain't got any more friends —if indeed they ever truly were —the only thing left is to be aware of your enemies…

I'm through with it, brother. I've got just as strong a will to live as anyone, but I also have a life sentence I haven't even started yet. I ain't going to do it being fucked with. And fuck all this shit about punishment and reward. When it's your time, it's your time. The next son of a bitch that plays this game with me is going to find out it's not as amusing as he thought it would be.

I appreciate your letter, Bo and Sita, and I appreciate the years of togetherness we've shared. I'm here, and your friend, Mickey

Call me demented —and you wouldn't be the first —but I love this letter from Mickey. In it he gives so many clues about where his pain is coming from: starting a life sentence, feeling that he has no friends, being ridiculed for sharing with others the thoughts and strategies that he's used to help himself, his epilepsy and more than likely, a feeling of having been abandoned by or having lost his friend Paul. He was facing, not only spending the rest of his life in prison, but spending it without his one close friend.

Mickey's anger surrounding Paul reminds me of the end of my freshman year in college. I lived in an all-women's dorm and about two weeks before the end of the school year, just about every woman in that dorm got into a fight with any other women with whom they were close —my roommate and I were among them. Some of us were headed to new universities and the rest of us were headed to other living arrangements around and off campus. We were not only facing a summer apart, but many of us would no longer be roommates. I remember realizing that we were fighting to make the separation and transition easier. We were finding reasons not to like each other so that we wouldn't miss each other so much.

Mickey not only had a true and caring friend in Paul, but someone who was like-minded. In Paul, Mickey had someone who respected and shared his spirituality and spiritual seeking, rather than ridiculing it. In Paul he had a soul brother. Mickey says that even today —thirty years later —"Most of my fellow inmates are involved in religions that are fear-based and don't relate well to my beliefs." With Paul, Mickey wasn't a freak or an outsider. He was simply a like-minded friend. When Paul was transferred, he left behind him a large and lonely void in Mickey's life. No wonder Mickey worked so hard to hate him.

This letter is also a testimony to the power of love. Mickey hasn't had a lot of kindness or care in his life and this letter shows that he holds on to it when it comes his way. Even as Mickey is expressing his contempt for Bo and Sita's beliefs, he is telling them that he is their friend, sending them warm greetings and believing –in the midst of some very strong paranoia –that because they had cared for him so much and for so long, they would not harm him.

In response to this letter from Mickey, Bo wrote a very long and caring letter. The following are Mickey's last two letters to Bo and Sita. They are a fantastic summary of the ups and extreme downs during this period of his life:

Dear Bo,

I received your letter. You said it pretty well. But then, you always have since I've known you. I wish I could put it into such perfect perspective. If I survive this drama, maybe someday I will.

I trust you, bro. I trust Sita, too. Anybody that cares, I've got to trust. And your letter wasn't a bunch of bullshit. That letter came from the heart. I've got two friends for life and maybe even after. There are millions who don't have that much. I am fortunate. I can't throw it away on some paranoid whim. Besides, where would I throw it? I once read that systems of energy contain no garbage. I still believe it. So where could it go?

I know you and Sita are busy, but I'd like to tell you a story: I used to walk the west yard a lot. I walked it for several years; walked it in the scorching summer, the icy snow, the drenching rain and walked it in the mellow days of May. I could make 350 laps a day easily. Sometimes made a thousand.

One day while I was walking, a fellow convict ambled up beside me and fell into step. After a few laps he said, "You wanna get high?" I said sure and he broke out five good joints. I smoked with him and I got very high and introspective, the way good smoke makes you.

I stopped walking and looked around. Suddenly I knew the score. I watched some blacks shucking and jiving like a Fleetwood on blocks, I checked out the poker tables, where guilt-ridden men threw away hundreds as fast as they could read their hands, and the hungry ate it up with relish. I saw the drag queens in their skin-tight pants and dark eye-liner made from magic markers, selling their wares for five packs a shot, I saw the young pretty ones, sitting alone, turned out against their will and their eyes were dead.

I saw the stabbings, the homicides, and the utter futility of someone making themselves a reputation, as if a brutal act would in some way make them more of what they already were. I killed once, as you know. I stabbed an innocent man 30 times and cut his throat. I felt guilty. I even attempted suicide several times, but the rope always seemed to break right as I was losing consciousness. I began to believe it just wasn't my time, so I blew it off.

The friend came by and turned me on to Be Here Now and Inside-Out and he also brought me a great deal of weed. I read the books a minimum of ten times each. Afterward, I would meditate and then smoke a joint. Next I would start my asanas. I got it together for the first time in my life and had it together for several years after that. In my heart something began to blossom and grow. For some reason I didn't even understand, there appeared an actual feeling of love and compassion.

For the first time in my life, I knew love —the kind you spoke of, the kind Sita spoke of. Yeah, I felt the bliss of forgetting myself long enough to remember my brothers. I was, it seems, in a form of Bhakti Yoga, damn near all the time.

But then came a time when my mother overdosed and died. She wasn't only a mother, but my best friend as well, and just about my only link to the outside world.

Not long after, my friend and lover for several years was transferred suddenly to another institution (I'm in the category of "no-choice bisexuality" because ain't nothing else possible) And though his departure meant little to most, it was devastating to me. I drew in other lovers to take away the hurt and became attached to each one and each one sooner or later was transferred away, each time hurting.

I became tired of it all and very bitter. The blossom in my heart began to fade and become choked. Fuck all of 'em. I figured I had just been used by all those people anyway. Well, now I would use and hurt people, in whatever way I could. I didn't think these exact words, consciously I was just trying to get numb, trying not to feel anything but indifference, if you can call that a feeling.

I almost succeeded. I talked bad about people, stole their dope and just generally violated every convict code imaginable. I had sunk to the very depths of hell, brother. The fact that I am still breathing is only due to some of these convicts' compassion. I know it in my heart. They don't use fifty-cent words or play the psychiatric game, but they care about me and they are sincere when they say, "I'm your friend and it hurts me to see you in this bad state." I know they are sincere, because I've made quite a habit of lying these past three years and can knock off someone else that's lying. Or at least I think I can.

My bitterness didn't quite work out like it thought it would. I ended up hurting only myself. And I think now I'm glad of that. I don't think I'm glad I'm hurting, but I'm glad I'm not hurting someone else. Not only because I'd feel even more guilty than I already have, but simply because I have a few friends who I never want to see hurt or misused. Could be that I'm learning about love, through the good times and the bad.

Thanks for your help, Bo. I don't know if anyone ever writes and tells you how much peace and love your words inspire, but believe me, they inspire probably more than you are aware of…

I hope I explained this story right. If I didn't, then just read the following:
I LOVE YOU, Mickey

(When Mickey said "read the following" he was referring to another loving letter that was enclosed with the one above. The two letters came together on a Monday. On Wednesday, just two days later, Bo received this next letter:)

Dear Bo and Sita,
Well, it is now thought by this writer to tell you that he sincerely hopes that you both will please disregard his two previous letters in which he expounded so much on the trickery of the mind.

It was a good ploy, but it won't do a thing for his difficulties. In fact is difficulties are even greater than they were then.

Disregard it all as a lie. No, not all of it. When he said he loved you, he still does. Or whatever it's called. He just ain't gonna be convinced that his mind has done anything but be what it is.

This writer will be going back to Easter State Hospital in the next few days. There they will fill his mind with psychotropic drugs and he will forget. He may even forget who he is, until someone says, "Mickey." Then he will say "oh."

He is now on the nut ward, and when you get this letter, he will have probably already be gone.

...Mickey would like to die more than anything. But he just doesn't have the courage to do it himself yet. Many people would like to see that occur, though. No, many people would rather just see him experience continual pain. Well, just fuck them and fuck you. [unsigned]

Mickey's letters tell us the story of three major losses over a short span: his mother died, his lover was transferred and his friend Paul was up for transfer as well. Mickey had so few bright spots in his life and the few that he had were taken from him in fairly rapid succession. No wonder he plummeted.

Mickey had not been in touch with Bo and Sita since these letters in the early eighties, but when he wrote me about them, he expressed much appreciation and affection for them. When I asked if he would like to donate proceeds from this book to any organizations, it was their Human Kindness Foundation (which still does prison outreach) that was first on his list. I felt sad that he no longer had a connection with them, especially since I assumed it had to do with Mickey's shame more than anything else. I emailed Sita and gave her Mickey's address and she emailed back saying that she wrote him a letter that very same day. When Mickey received her letter, he wrote to me saying, "I received a letter from Sita today. You must have given her my address. I am overwhelmed. It has been twenty-seven years." They have now resumed correspondence and I feel happy for having meddled.

Mickey told me that he didn't keep in touch with Bo and Sita because they no longer do the same kind of prison programs. My assumption is that he no longer wrote them for the same reason that he didn't initially include this chapter of his life in his story. It's a chapter that he'd rather not revisit and remember. It's a chapter of his life for which he's not particularly proud --and in a life full of actions and decisions for which he is not proud, this says something.

In Mickey's original manuscript he mentioned epilepsy only once. It was in the chapter about quitting school and he said: "I had epilepsy and wasn't athletic." That's all. He lumped having epilepsy and not being athletic together as if they were on par in terms of their impact on his social, emotional and academic wellbeing.

I sensed that Mickey was trying to breeze past the subject of epilepsy, which told me that for him epilepsy wasn't at all a breezy topic. I asked him to write about a time in which he had a seizure that was especially hard on him or that was especially pivotal in the way the world treated him. I asked this many times over the course of several of months and finally got, not a story, but the couple of sentences about epilepsy that are written in his chapter about quitting school. Mickey wants to talk about his epilepsy as much as he wants to talk about his bouts of paranoia —not at all. Both conditions have tormented him, made him feel ashamed and caused others to fear him and think less of him. Both are conditions that have kept love at a distance.

Humans are basically herd animals and when members of a herd feel that one of their own is somehow "not right," somehow out of alignment, they assume that whatever makes that member out of alignment also makes it more vulnerable to predators. Because of this, they keep that member at a distance. They don't want to be collateral damage when the wolf comes for it.

Even though we no longer have to worry much about being prey for wolves, and even though safety no longer necessarily comes in numbers, that mechanism is still part of our cellular makeup. It is a natural reaction to keep people who are vulnerable (people whose marriages are crumbling, their finances or self-esteem spiraling, their health failing, their fears getting the best of them) out of our herds. Mickey's vulnerability wasn't just sensed by the herd; it was right out there writhing on the floor out of control.

Mickey's paranoia has been even more distressing to the herd than his brief out-of-control seizures. Fear causes us to go into fight-or-flight mode. It shuts down the cerebral cortex, where reason resides, and puts the most ancient and low-functioning part of our brain, the "reptile brain," into the driver's seat. Fear makes us do incredibly stupid things and the last thing the herd wants is for one of its members to be doing incredibly stupid things. We fear our fear and we fear the fear of others. We fear fear more than anything else. In Mickey's fear we see fear run amuck. We see our fears come to life. Mickey's "fuck you"s trigger our flight response and we, the herd, stampede away.

Mickey must look at me, with my long-term happy marriage, two sweet kids, higher education, financial stability and complete lack of criminal record, as a solid member of the herd, someone safe and secure and in alignment with my in-alignment peers. He must look at me as being like "them" more than him. Most of all, he must see me as someone who couldn't possibly understand or empathize. But this is what makes this part of Mickey's life so powerful. We can all empathize. We've all been outside the herd at times and even more often have imagined ourselves to be. Many of us spend much of our effort trying to look acceptable and in-alignment enough to be kept within the safety of our herd.

Because of childhood trauma, I began seeing the world through adult-like lenses while still residing in a little girl's body. I did not share the same idealism and optimism about our herd as my young peers. This made me out of alignment. There was something "not right" about me. Parents raised their eyebrows at the too-mature things I said. My peers had no idea what to do with me. I was kept at the outer reaches of the herd until almost high school, when I suddenly became an internal match for my outward age. From that point on I have been safely in the herd. But those of us who spend a great deal of time outside it, especially during our formative years, never fully feel a part of the herd. I believe this is by design. In not fully feeling connected with the herd, I've come to feel deeply connected with Life, with God, with The Force, with whatever you want to call this beautiful thing of which we are all a part. Mickey has too —and we then form our own kind of herd.

Those of us who have been outside the herd at one point or another —meaning every single one of us —can relate to Mickey's outsider status. The emotional wounds he experienced from being an outsider bring up our own similar emotional wounds and we get a chance to nurture and heal them a little.

Within all of us is an outcast, a freak, an outsider —and most definitely someone who is sometimes very afraid. In Mickey's story is a little bit of our story. In Mickey's healing is a little bit of healing for all of us.

Free and Foolish

The following year I was assigned to a job and a different housing unit. I was appointed work in the mattress factory and moved to the newly renovated F Cell House. The F Cell house held 3 inmates to a cell, and was large by prison standards. My cell mates were named Stan and David and we got along well.

The mattress factory was located behind the prison walls, but it too was surrounded by fences, razor wire and gun towers.

I spent my time stitching ACA jail pads and within a month became proficient.

I enjoy hard work. It is satisfying and proves to be a distraction from the mundane and mediocre idleness of prison.

One morning a truck towing a horse trailer entered the industrial area and backed up to the loading dock of the mattress factory. They were there to pick up a consignment of 100 mattresses for a state agency. We were left alone with our duties while the supervisor and truck driver wandered to the mess hall for coffee. A co-worker and I were appointed the task of loading the truck.

An inmate who worked with me and who was serving a life sentence dreamed up an escape scheme that he thought might work. He asked us to fill the trailer with mattresses and then he'd place himself beneath them. We agreed to it, but I had little faith that his endeavor would succeed.

Every truck leaving the prison was driven into a sallyport, an area in-between two locked gates. At the sallyport the undercarriage of the truck was checked with mirrors and a large iron pole was shoved around and between the jail pads.

I thought it a foolish attempt, but I watched from a window as the truck made it through the sallyport and out into the free world with its passenger stowed away.

Luck was with him. I let out the breath I had been holding.

The fellow was out only briefly. He was caught two days later in Oklahoma City, after robbing a woman at gunpoint. She quickly called the police.

The day after his capture my co-worker and I were fired from the mattress factory. Our boss was dismissed, as well. It seems we all came away losers from the scenario and I was angry at my fellow inmate for so abusing his chance at freedom.

Another time, I was sitting at a table in the yard and witnessed a most brazen escape. The yard was surrounded by tall walls and one guard tower, yet in broad daylight, a young man scurried up the side of the cell house, using the bars as a ladder until he got to the roof. From there he made his way to the roof of the administration building and jumped to his freedom. The tower was no more than one hundred yards from him, but they never noticed him.

Before he'd jumped the wall, he'd cut the picture of a large foot from a magazine and glued it to cardboard. He then placed it at the end of his bunk, sticking out from under his blanket. He put clothes under the blanket to make it look like someone was sleeping there. When the guards passed by for count, they saw the fake foot and counted him as being there.

He was gone about thirty-six hours before they discovered his ruse. He lasted six months on the outside before being arrested for bank robbery in Florida. I thought the man was such a fool. I knew that when I was released (in those days it was still "when" and not "if") I would savor everything about it. I would make a life for myself in the free world and it would be all the more wonderful because I had learned to appreciate everything about it. Turns out, when it was my turn for freedom, I was no better at handling it than the others. I too was a fool.

Killed for a Canned Ham

In 1983 I had been in prison ten years and once again my custody level dropped from maximum to medium and they transferred me to a lower security prison called Conner Correctional Center.

Conner was located in the northeastern part of the state, near Tulsa, Oklahoma. It was designed in a way that I had never seen before.

There were no bars or large walls with gun towers; there was only one tower located in the front of the prison, and two fences topped with razor wire.

The housing units were unlike cell houses. Each unit held two Quadrants, separated by a short, concrete sidewalk, each Quad held two tiers, two on one side of the building, two on the other; each with a glassed-in control center that operated the opening of the doors.

The doors were solid steel with a small, slit window in the center. The cells were designed for two men. The back wall had a horizontal window but it would only open a maximum of six inches.

The prison held five of these units, each with its own dining room.

Outside the units there was no yard to speak of; however, there was a large ball field behind the facility and the gate to it was usually left open.

I arrived in August, 1983; the dog days of summer. The cells were like ovens. There were no cooling vents to circulate the air in the cells. The only air circulation was through the six inch window.

I met several inmates whom I had done time with at OSP and luck had it that I was transferred to the same prison as Paul and we were in the same unit. Two other good friends were there and we immediately made up our own little group and stayed to ourselves.

From the first day I sensed a tension and discontent on the yard. It was hot, tempers were short and some of the COs were physical and violent.

The tension came to a head, and then ruptured, three weeks after my arrival.

The main kitchen sent hamburgers for dinner to all the units save one. They ran out of burgers and substituted a vile-smelling casserole. The cons who received the casserole became enraged, threw their trays against the walls of the dining hall and seized the CO's as hostages.

It took only an hour for word of what was happening to reach the other buildings. The other inmates did not hesitate to follow suit. They shattered the glass of the Control Centers and took the guards hostage.

I had flashbacks to the riot of 1973 and knew this would not be good.

My friends and I armed ourselves with clubs taken from the destroyed control centers. Having learned how violent and dangerous prison riots can be, I gathered my friends into my cell this time and kept them from participating. One of my friends produced a full bag of marijuana. We were afraid, full of adrenaline and happy to have something that would help to soften the sharp edges of our circumstance. We got very stoned. If we were to endure the violence and deprivation of a full blown riot, we were going to do it as comfortably as possible.

Living in a unit across the yard from mine was a young friend named Bo, who was originally from South Dakota. Prior to the riot he had made a deal with me for a gallon of pruno. My friends and I talked it over and agreed that Paul and I would make the journey to Bo's cell and recover the alcohol. There was a great deal of mayhem on the yard, but we felt safe with our clubs and marijuana fogged brains.

We left the unit and hastily made our way across the yard which was dark except for the light of fires burning in the dining halls. We did not run into trouble. Most were concerned with their own agendas.

We made it to Bo's cell and he welcomed us with the one gallon of pruno in a plastic trash bag. I thanked him and we took our leave.

On the return journey we ran into trouble. Snipers lay on the roofs of the administration buildings and were taking pot shots at a group of young inmates. The inmates hurled rocks at the shooters and then dived behind the brick walls of the chapel. Pieces of mortar and brick were flying. It was total chaos.

To make it back to our unit we would have to pass through this barrage of gunfire. "Hey fellas!" I yelled to the rock hurling inmates, "We have hostages and we've got to safely get through. Give us a break!" The ruse worked and they left us alone. The gunfire had also gone silent. We hurriedly passed through.

Later that night the world turned tragic. Bo, the young man from whom I had gotten the pruno drank too much and ventured onto the palazzo in a drunken state, heading for the kitchen in search of food. He found a canned ham and while leaving the kitchen did not heed the orders from the Riflemen to drop it. He was summarily executed with a bullet to the head.

Hearing of the event, being mindful of the snipers, I hesitantly made my way to the kitchen. I saw him face-down, part of his head erased, yet still clutching the canned ham. I felt a rush of sorrow. He was twenty years old and in prison only because he'd been in possession of a few drugs while passing through Oklahoma. He'd only had a three-year sentence and had been killed over a canned ham. My friends and I spoke little for the remainder of the night.

The next morning, my friends and I left our cell without shirts, just as the voice coming over the loudspeaker ordered us to do. As soon as we exited the Quad, we saw National Guard soldiers everywhere, along with an armed contingent of State Troopers. We were ordered to form a line and march to the ball field. A group of inmates came out of the building carrying a white sheet attached to a broom handle. It was surreal.

The line of inmates was long and some were poked and prodded in the side with carbines as the line snaked along. I said nothing, nor did Paul, who was directly in front of me. We marched in silence.

We were forced to sit silently on the grass of the ball field for most of the morning.

Around noon we were handcuffed and placed in leg irons. We shuffled to military buses idling in front of the prison. Paul and I sat next to one another, with our friends in the seat behind us. The air conditioner malfunctioned and it was unbearably hot. The windows did not open. We were told we were being transferred to Oklahoma State Prison (OSP).

When we arrived at OSP we were placed in the West Cell house which had been condemned and emptied of inmates for some time, but they had nowhere else to put us, so this was our new home. We were in two-man cells, Paul and I in one, our two friends next to us. Our friend had smuggled in the weed and we stayed stoned with our neighbors most of the time. It helped pass the time while we were locked down twenty-four hours a day.

Kim
(The Book of Paul)

I meddled in Mickey's social life a second time by looking for Mickey's best friend Paul. After reading Paul's letters and seeing his strong support role in Mickey's life during that time, I became curious about what had become of him. Paul and Mickey had been soul brothers and up until that time, the closest friends that either had ever had. I was motivated to see them reconnected. It was incomprehensible to me that such close friends had allowed themselves to lose contact with each other and I wanted to remedy that.

I wrote Mickey asking for Paul's last name, but mail was taking three weeks or more to get to Mickey, so I decided to email Sita to see if she knew how to reach Paul. She responded with an email that started with "Kim, you're going to love this..." and then pasted an email she had recently received from Paul after about nine years of no contact from him. The "coincidence" of Paul contacting Sita shortly before I contacted her looking for him was not lost on me. And it turns out that Paul was born and raised in Tulsa and had just been working in Tulsa before moving to Wisconsin to reunite with his wife and adult children. I had just missed meeting him in person.

I left a phone message for Paul and he left a message back saying, "Anyone who is in contact with Mickey Owens is someone I am excited to talk to!" When we did connect by phone, I had the same reaction to our call that I had when I first connected with Mickey. It didn't feel like a first meeting, but like a continuation of something. Paul has a low, slow voice with the very slight southern drawl of most Oklahomans. It's a voice made for lullabies or Mark Cohn songs. He plays acoustic guitar, writes his own songs and when he was out of prison the last round, performed his music in bars with a couple of other musicians. He recently saved up enough for a guitar and is getting back into his music.

The last several years of prison, Paul worked as the assistant to the prison clergyman. He feels called to go back into the prisons and serve in some way, perhaps doing kindness trainings, but the specific avenue hasn't yet come to him.

Paul has two goals in life at this point: to make it as a free man and to repair and build relationships with his ex-wife and with his children, who are now in their early twenties. Paul wasn't there for much of his children's lives, nor to help his wife raise two children and help make ends meet. He's got a lot of reparation and trust-building work to do with his family. They are, very reasonably, wary, hurt and angry. He gets emotional when he talks about them and his voice often breaks. He brags about his kids and is so impressed with the people they've become.

At the age of fifty-three Paul was released from a nine year stint in prison into an economy in which people without criminal records were having trouble finding work. He had served a total of thirty-one years in correctional institutions. His criminal record, age and the economy were all big hurdles to finding a job, but his brother pulled through for him and got him work in Tulsa. With that job Paul built credibility and headed to Wisconsin to reunite with his family and find a job on his own.

He's been temping fulltime for a paper packing company and the people there have been impressed with his work ethic and are looking at making him a fulltime company employee. He has pride in his voice when he talks about how hard he works and how impressed the company is with his work. When he was on the outside previously, he had developed his own computer sales and service company and did some programming on the side as well. He said he did pretty well with it and wants to go to a technical school to get certification so that he can do it again and be more credible to potential clients. This told me that he had taught himself computer programming –which told me that he, like Mickey, is whip-smart.

Paul followed up our first phone call with an email. What he wrote and the way he expressed himself was so similar to Mickey's letters that it was easy to see why they were such close friends. Paul told me that Mickey was the closest friend he'd ever had in prison and that even after twenty-seven years, he still considered him one of his best friends.

As alike as Paul and Mickey are, they are strikingly different in a way. Paul has a "the world is going to hell in a hand basket" view of the world. He sees the bad things that people are doing and what is going wrong. He sees the world as having fallen from Grace. Mickey sees the Grace, the innate good, in just about everyone and everything. Mickey once said, "You think I had a hard childhood, well Paul has me beat." I assume that

Paul is not yet ready or able to forgive the experiences and people who have wounded him. Mickey has (over and over again) done his forgiveness work and by doing so has created the room for light to flow into his spirit and experience—and then out from him into the world. They are two beautiful souls with very similar minds focused on opposite sides of the coin.

A little later in our email correspondence, Paul sent me a poem he had recently written and I was again struck by how like-minded Paul and Mickey are :

Zenishness

Contemplation of a single point
while focused on nothing –
before and after are non-existent.
uual
A fleeting glimpse by the ego
of a moment that neither begins
nor ends.

Gazing into an identity-less procession
of nobody's anywhere.

Un-graspable fractions
of a conceptual withdrawal
within a vacuum of perpetual change.

Fully cognizant while completely detached
seeing everything everywhere
in no time or space.

Beginingless-ness always brings everything

total emptiness is full of all knowledge.

Completely comprehending the vanity of
understanding
while nothing is happening where everything begins.

The finite boasts a"yes"as the infinite shakes a"no"
as the present nods its approval of
the never.

Always incomplete is the conclusive blissful thrill
of anyone's enlightenment.

Everybody's endless activeness ceaselessly deludes us
all
until nothingness empties of its everything.

Then is separateness known to be foolishness
the resulting illusion causing laughter to bring great
pain!

— Paul Hays (Circa: In Eternity)

Paul called me the day that he received his first letter
from Mickey in twenty-seven years and he was so
moved by it that he cried. He said that Mickey's words
inspired him and I was so happy that the two of them
were reunited. A month after making initial contact
with Paul I got a letter from Mickey wondering why
Paul hadn't yet written to him. He was not only
perplexed, but hurt. I had been writing Mickey, telling
him about the long phone conversations Paul and I
had been having and how I wished that he and I could

have long phone conversations. I wrote him about the things Paul teased me about. I wrote him about Paul's struggles, how hard he was working to make it and how at one point he seemed to teeter on the edge. I wrote all of this assuming that Mickey was getting similar letters from Paul.

When I found out that Paul wasn't writing Mickey I became like a mother lion. I roared. As far as I was concerned there was no excuse for not having written and I came down on Paul really hard. He pushed back with impressive intensity, saying "You have no idea what I'm going through or what my life is like. You are not in my shoes" —which was true. And so it was that just a month into our friendship, Paul and I had our first fight and Mickey was already deeply hurt —and I discovered that Paul was going to upset the apple cart of our emotional lives just as much as Mickey and I had done with each other. This wasn't going to be just a warm fuzzy kumbaya triad. The three of us were going to push each other to grow some more.

I asked Paul if he wanted to share any stories about Mickey and he sent the following:

Mickey and I met each other when we were side-by-side in administrative segregation cells. I heard his voice before I saw his face. He struck me as somebody trying to find a friend. We struck up conversation easily and the topic quickly moved to spiritual matters. I immediately perceived him as someone who could see deeper into things and into people than the average person. He looked at life way beyond the common viewpoint. Both of us recognized each other as true seekers. We could tell we were both seeking something beyond what most others are satisfied with.

I was new to Ad-Seg and so looked to him to explain how it worked and what was expected of us. I was also relatively new to prison, so he was my prison mentor and very soon became my spiritual mentor as well. I was twenty-four years old and had never before encountered someone like Mickey, someone who would offer guidance, especially about spiritual matters.

Mickey was well thought of. No one ever said a negative thing about him, except when he went through a bad time, got angry and did things that seemed intended to get people angry at him. At the time, I wondered if he was trying to get himself killed, because he was in a very dark place. But even doing the things he did, no one harmed him. They were tolerant of him. Men in prison get beaten or even killed for some of the things that Mickey did when he went off the deep end. But they knew he was just going through a really bad time.

He didn't smile much, unless he was sharing something humorously enlightening and he was not open except with people who were his close friends, but with that handful of people he was emotionally intimate.

Mickey had dark very curly hair that he kept slightly long and parted in the middle. He didn't strut or try to appear tough. His manner was relaxed and natural and by prison standards, approachable. Mickey isn't a big guy (only about 5' 7" and small-framed) and he was just a kid when he entered one of the worst prisons in the country at one of the worst times for prisons. He had to quickly learn how to protect himself and how to survive in that hard and violent environment.

Once we were out of Ad-Seg and free to go into the yard we got into running. Mickey was into running and got me into it. We'd jog around the yard and talk. It was a tight loop and we got kind of dizzy.

We were in different cell blocks, but for a long time we met at the same table at the same time for breakfast every morning. It was a daily ritual that we both really looked forward to, the highlight of our days. But one day at breakfast —I was there first and waiting at the table for him —I saw him come through the door and into the dining line and noticed something different about his posture and his gestures. And then I noticed that he got into an argument with one of the line servers. I had never seen him argue with anyone.

When he had filled his tray, he went to a table all by himself instead of meeting at our table. He was hunched like he had the weight of the world on his shoulders. When I finally caught his eye, he gave me a really dirty look. I had never seen anything like that from Mickey. It was intimidating, but he was still my friend and I wasn't going to tolerate him avoiding me and needed to know what was going on. I moved my tray and sat across from him. He looked up at me with his eyes, but not his head. He kept his chin pointed toward his tray and said something like "what the hell do you want?" He gave me a long spiel about how I was like everyone else in that prison. He thought I was scheming against him. I was upset that my best friend was talking to me like that and walked away. But I didn't let his behavior scare me. I didn't feel afraid of him.

This was the time in which I wrote the letters to Bo and Sita that are published in their book. Mickey sliced his neck and was hospitalized in a psychiatric unit. The emotional and mental state he was in crushed me with all the pain. I felt like I had lost my best friend. I was angry at him for turning on me like that, but I knew it had to do with things beyond his control and I was determined to stay his friend and bring him back to sanity.

He went to a psychiatric facility and I didn't see him for months. When he was discharged he was sent to a different prison and it wasn't until months after that that I was relocated to the same facility. It wasn't quite the same between Mickey and me for a long time. But we were still bonded well enough that when the riot occurred I was concerned about him and searched for him. We did not engage in any violence, but we stood our ground. Out of the nine hundred inmates, there were one hundred and thirteen men who refused to surrender during the riot and Mickey and I were two of them. The conditions were horrible and we refused to quit before some kind of commitment toward improvements were made. The National Guard finally gained access to the prison and forced us out of the yard naked at gunpoint where we were placed in jumpsuits and then on buses to a condemned cell at OSP-- because there was no room for us in the regular prison. We were given an option regarding who we wanted to cell with and Mickey and I chose to cell together. That was when Mickey and I became cellmates and we again became very close.

During the years that I had known him, Mickey had never once talked about having killed a man, but I witnessed how he struggled emotionally. Mickey was on a prescription drug that helped alleviate the side effects of another prescription drug that he was on. When this drug was taken in excess, it acted as a hallucinogen. We were in our cell one day and he took a whole handful of those pills and offered some to me too. I didn't handle them very well, nor did Mickey. He paced back and forth in the cell for what may have been hours, singing the same song over and over again. I finally yelled at him to stop and he stopped pacing and began sobbing. He spilled the whole story about

*having killed a man along with a guilt that seemed bottomless.
He said, "That man didn't do anything to me. He was innocent.
I can never take that back. I can't bring him back..." He went
on crying and talking until he was spent and I just sat there
quietly and let him do it. I tried to console him and let him know
that he was forgiven, that the powers in the Spiritual realm were
very aware that he didn't mean to do what he did, that his fears
pushed him to do something he wouldn't have otherwise done. He
acted like he didn't want to hear what I had to say. He didn't
want to excuse himself, he just wanted to grieve. Once it was
over, we never talked about it again.*

*Mickey helped me see the world differently and opened me to new
beliefs about life and God that have supported me through many
hard times. I served twenty-five calendar years in prison and he
was the best friend I ever had while serving time.*

*Toward the end of my time in prison with Mickey, I was heavily
involved in a campaign to get nutritious meals served to the
inmates and later, at another prison, I started a prison
newspaper. I think Mickey resented how much time these projects
took away from our friendship and he distanced himself from me.
When I was released I gave Mickey my home phone number and
invited him to call me collect. He called me and we had nice
conversations until things in my life and marriage fell apart and
I got preoccupied with the mess, moved to another place and
another phone number and Mickey and I never talked again
after that. It has been about twenty-seven years since I've spoken
to him and when Kim left me a message that she was calling me
about "Mickey Owens," I was very excited about reconnecting
with my old friend. When I got my first letter from him, I was so
moved that I cried. His words inspired me, just like they did
twenty-seven years ago. Mickey reminds me of the person I am
and can be. He also talked about Kim and I'll share what he*

wrote about her, because I got a good laugh from it and because I
agree with him:

"Kim printed out the email that you sent her and my first thought was: how the hell did she find you? The woman is tenacious, bro, and like a dog with a bone she won't let go until she finds what she's looking for. But she has a heart as large as the moon and she is a wonderful and loving person . . ."

Dear Kim,

I look through my narrow window and watch the cars and trucks pass on the highway. I wonder where they are going and what they think as they pass this place. Do they think we are monsters? Are they grateful that we are safely locked away from them? Do they imagine what it would be like to live here? Odds are they don't give us much thought at all. One thing is for sure, they don't think they could ever end up in a place like this...

Dear Mickey,

I have passed dozens upon dozens of prisons in my moves and travels and have never acclimated to them. I cannot pass one without feeling profoundly sad. There are always signs that say, "Do not pick up hitchhikers." It cracks me up that someone thought people might be tempted to pick up a hitchhiker right outside a prison. I would freak out if I saw a hitchhiker outside a prison. But I have always been tempted to stop and look for signs of life, to catch some clues about what it is like there and what the people are like. I wonder about the stories of the men or women —or youth—in those places. I wonder what reverse alchemy of circumstance and psychology came together that brought them there. For miles and miles after I pass a prison, a cloud of melancholy hovers in me. But you are right; I have never thought I could end up where you are. Prison has seemed as much a possibility for me as going to the moon.

Supposedly our brains —and subsequently our world views and psychological foundations —are almost completely hardwired by the age of three. This means that you and I were almost completely formed by circumstances that we don't remember. I think about you as a baby and a toddler and what it was you saw in your father that formed your view of what a man should

145

be and what you experienced that formed your impression about what adults should be and what to expect from life. I think about what you experienced that formed your impression of who you are and how you fit into the world. It's not fair that we are programmed so young and by forces so completely out of our control. But then, I suppose that's how it goes with all of life. We're thrown into the current at birth and do our best to flow with it. If we do really well, we learn to relax and enjoy the ride. The fact that you seem to be able to do that —more than most of us "free" folks anyway —is really something.

A hug to you over the airwaves,
Kim

In an "Articulate Manner"

One night, after about a year back at OSP, Paul and I were rudely awakened by a loud, crashing noise. Several shouted voices echoed around the Dayroom. I could not make out the words, and seeing that all the doors were ajar, including ours, I came out to investigate.

I saw a group of inmates, perhaps ten or fifteen, gathered around the soda machine, which had been toppled over. Several convicts were using knives to pry open the back of the machine. Metal was torn away, and the group shouted triumphantly as cans of soda were removed and passed around.

I did not ask myself where the guards were. I could see that the Control Centers glass had been shattered and it was empty. This was becoming old hat for me, another riot.

I saw a group of convicts come out of a cell with the guard hostages in tow. The guards were manacled in chains and leg irons.

There were six hostages, and the convicts guarding them were moving from cell to cell in case a sniper zeroed in on them through the narrow confines of the windows in someone's cell. I did not care to be involved in any of it and stayed in my cell. But that would change in the coming night.

Because writing and reading came easily to me, I had begun using my time writing letters for cons who were illiterate and helping inmates file grievances. I also acted as a peacekeeper between inmates and helped diffuse violence wherever I could. I got a lot of fulfillment doing this and also gained a reputation as someone who could speak well and give voice to issues. Because of this, two of my good friends came to my cell and said there was a line open to a radio station on one of the telephones and urged me to talk to the DJ and air some of our grievances in "an articulate manner." I said I would. What the hell, I didn't like how the prison was being run either.

I said hello to the disk jockey and expressed our grievances and the discontent we felt in this new prison; rarely any outdoor exercise, and that which was provided was a joke; too small to work out, too crowded to even walk.

The food was disgusting, and the small portions doled out were causing us to lose weight.

Use of the law library was limited to only those who had court deadlines. A CO made arbitrary decisions on who would use it and who not.

The lack of jobs resulted in boring idleness and frustration for many of the inmates.

Medical care was almost non-existent. Unless an inmate was on his deathbed, he went untreated and ignored.

Sure, we were convicts, and most of us were guilty for what we were in prison for, but we were still human beings and all we were asking was to be treated humanely.

I further added that the hostages were being treated far better than they treated us. I told them that there was no violence, at least in our Quad, and that this incident was not meant for destruction, but to hopefully bring our grievances to those who would listen.

I was about to say goodbye when the DJ asked me my name. Fearing retribution I answered that I was just a "concerned convict." I then walked away and went back to my cell. They would be retaking the prison soon, and I wanted to be in my cell when they did.

They came at dawn. The hostages had been released, again on promises that were never kept. There was no further reason to avoid the inevitable.

Tear gas canisters were fired into the Quad and anyone left standing out there was ordered to lie face down on the floor. Everyone complied. It was not long before the gas had everyone choking. Once in the Dayroom they ordered every inmate to return to his cell, and made no attempt to hurt anyone. I was surprised. Probably because there were news crews nearby.

The cell doors were shut and locked. They would not open again for two months.

Christmas

As dysfunctional as my family was, my mom and later my stepdad too, made sure that we had happy holidays during our childhood. Teresa and I dressed up for Halloween and were taken trick-or-treating. My favorite costume was Casper the Ghost, a costume that is probably no longer in existence today. For Thanksgiving we'd go to my grandma's house and have the traditional big meal with extended family. Christmas was my favorite holiday. We were always short on money, but my parents made sure we had at least one wrapped gift on Christmas morning. My memories of holidays are happy memories.

When I first entered prison, holidays and Christmases in particular were very sad and depressing times for me. I longed to be with my family. In prison, holidays mean even fewer privileges because the prison is short staffed. In maximum security prison we are normally locked down during holidays and unable to leave our cells at all. Apart from a meal that mildly resembles the real holiday meal, there is nothing celebratory about holidays in prison. After a while, I came to resent holidays and the decrease in privileges that came with them. I saw them as an annoyance. I became a scrooge. It was easier for me to feel this way.

I have one memory of a holiday in prison that brings a smile…It was the Christmas of 1986 and my neighbor in the next cell beat on the wall. I walked over to my food slot, which was elevated and welded to the corner of my cell.

"Reach over here with your hand," I heard him say. I

stuck my arm through the slot and touched his hand. He placed what felt like a cigarette in my palm. Withdrawing my arm, I opened my hand. In it lay a fat joint of marijuana. "Thank you very much, bro," I said. "Merry Christmas!" he said in return. I smiled the whole day.

Kim

We received a Christmas card from Mickey. This gesture touched me on so many levels: The normalcy of Mickey sending holiday cards just like everyone else and the incongruence of a festive card originating from such a grim location. I had difficulty picturing a selection of Holiday cards in a maximum security commissary. But most of all, it touched me that Mickey was sending cheer ("Merry Christmas Kim! I hope this day is joyful for you and your family! ") at a time when he would be on lockdown due to short staff and surrounded by the same concrete and steel, instead of loved ones and giving. I imagine the holidays are a strong reminder of what he does not have, that this time of year is when the contrast between the free world and his life in prison is most stark. I got a little choked up as I placed his card on the wall with the other holiday cards.

There is little that I am allowed to send Mickey, so the kids and I put together a simple Christmas packet for him with a few items we knew would pass security. He wrote me after receiving the packet, saying:

Dear Kim, I received your card, family photo (which is now taped to my wall) and the kids' beautiful drawings. You all get a giant hug from me! I wrote the kids a little story that I hope they are old enough to understand —never lose hope no matter what the world thinks of you. You are still God's child and are precious in His sight."

The Weed—for Ben and Eliza
In the beginning was the weed and the weed knew itself as strong and hearty. It grew everywhere one could see.

When the weed was blown by the wind its seeds scattered and took root. When the rain came it was beautiful and multiplied.

But then humans came and they did not like the weed. They said, "Weed, you must be gone. You do not belong here." And the weed answered, "But I was here first."

"Not anymore, weed," they said and tried to make it go away.

One day the weed was weeping, tears of pain running down its spiky stalk.

A nearby tree said, "Weed, why do you weep?"

And the weed answered, "Because I am ugly."

"Ugly?" the tree said, "Who told you, you were ugly?"

"People did," cried the weed.

"Well I do not think you're ugly," said the tree, "even though you choke my roots when you are angry."

"Easy for you to be so kind," pouted the weed. "People think you are lovely and majestic. They will never bother you."

"Oh?" answered the tree, "Ever heard of firewood?"

At this they laughed and both felt better.

So it was that the weed did not give up hope and still grows heartily to this very day.

And for Kim:

Bhakti

In every rose
And sunset
Does love appear
In tangled moss
And cobwebs
It does adhere…
In morning's light
Her smile's a song
Spirit of faith
To her belongs
Unfettered dreams
And love that sings
Of life and things
Mickey

[I didn't know the word "Bhakti" and so looked it up online. Here's what was said: "in Hinduism, Bhakti teaches the path of love and devotion as opposed to the path of knowledge. Bhakti is the expression of love and adoration centered upon the Supreme Person.]

Free at Last

My days at OSP were coming to an end and my custody level fell again to that of medium. I was transferred to Joseph Harp Correctional Center JHCC in the south central part of the State, near Oklahoma City. JHCC was the sister facility to Connor. They were built with the same layout, identical.

JHCC was one of the most liberally run prisons in the State. This was due in great measure to the Warden and his more enlightened policies. We were allowed to sell pizzas that the Jaycees made and we could wear our own clothing.

It was here that I began what would become a life-long daily meditation practice. I had meditated before, but this is when I incorporated it into my daily living. It became as much a part of my life as sleeping and waking. I would arise each morning before dawn and sit in the lotus position (which I had learned from practicing hatha yoga) and begin focusing on my breath as it entered and left out the tip of my nose. I would count my breaths until I reached two hundred. My mind would quiet and my pulse slowed way down. Deep into it I would sometimes see colors and hear sounds that I did not normally see and hear. Coming out of meditation I felt at peace and present and was able to go through my day more calm and aware. Sometimes I would do an imagery meditation and picture myself in a boat in a still mountain lake, surrounded by pine trees and their rich scent. I would look into the water and it was so clear that I could see all the way to the bottom.

My meditation practice has recharged me when I've felt depleted, renewed my hope when I've felt hopeless and calmed me when I've been agitated. It has had a more positive impact on my mental and emotional health than any drug ever prescribed for me.

During this time I had a job cleaning the dining hall and the sidewalk around it. I had learned that it's not so much what we're doing, but how we're being while doing it, so I did my job happily and well and because of that derived satisfaction from it.

The years passed at JHCC and were for the most part uneventful; days filled with the normal tedium and sameness inherent in all prisons. In 1991 the Federal District Court made a sweeping decision regarding the way Oklahoma applied its sentencing for the crime of 2nd Degree Murder. The Court ruled that an indeterminate sentence of ten years to life was in error. This happened to be the sentence that I had received back in 1977 and that I was currently serving.

I had a good friend on the yard named Thom. He and I had done time together for years at OSP and he was one of the most intelligent "jailhouse lawyers" (an inmate who knows the law) I'd ever known. I took my questions to him and asked if he'd help me.

He said he'd heard about the new ruling and that it was retroactive, meaning it went all the way back to 1976, when the crime was perpetrated. He agreed to file a petition on my behalf in Federal Court, in return for some essays he needed written. I was happy to do them.

Within a month the Court granted my petition and ordered the lower court to resentence me.

In early April, 1991, I was transported to the Pittsburgh County Courthouse in McAlester, Oklahoma. Once there, I anxiously awaited the Judge's entrance into the courtroom. My palms were sweating.

The Judge arrived and seated himself on the dais. It was Judge Robert Laydon, the same Judge who had given me the life sentence fifteen years earlier.

He asked me if I was aware of the latitude of the ranges in which he could sentence me – up to life.

I nodded and said "yes sir."

"Well," he continued, "I am instead going to sentence you to the minimum of ten years. Your crime is paid."

I wanted to cry with joy. Ten years! That would nearly put me out, I almost had that done!

Once back at JHCC they took me to classification to calculate my time. It turned out that I only had two months left to fulfill a ten year sentence. June 7, 1991 would be my freedom date.

I found Thom on the yard and told him the good news. After eighteen years (exactly half my life) I was going home.

Two months later I left the prison with my dress-out clothes and discharge papers. A female sergeant volunteered to drive me to the bus station in Oklahoma City. She liked me and I had always found her personality attractive and her looks too, with raven hair and green eyes that looked right into my heart and saw me, not an inmate, but *me*. As I passed through the last gate, I found myself in a parking lot. There were no guards but her, no chains or leg irons to restrain me. I was free.

There is nothing comparable to the joy and excitement I felt being free after spending almost two decades in prison. It was overwhelming, like a drowning man being pulled free of the water and suddenly filling his lungs with air. It was like a child taking his first bite of candy. I wanted to laugh at the clouds, to run wildly down the street shouting, "I'm here! I'm back! I got the brass ring!" for the first time in many years I laughed without fear of censure. I did not look back.

I got in the car and we sped away, me sitting, not in the back, but next to her in the passenger seat where it was appropriate for free people to sit.

Out on the highway it began to rain and she activated the windshield wipers. Even those were for me a symbol of freedom. The rain beat down relentlessly on the roof, but it was a different rain than what I had experienced in prison. It too was free and I would've gladly stood in it with my head bent back and mouth open to catch the drops and taste their freedom.

Once at the bus station I bought a ticket and the

sergeant and I sat in a booth in the refreshment center and drank coffee. "How're you feeling Mickey" she asked. "Great!" I answered, although I must admit that I was feeling anxious. I felt how open and vulnerable life was in the free world. People darted here and there without being told where to go. There seemed to be no reason for their haste, but I assumed that I was simply out of touch. Maybe I would understand in time. Time. I cared little for that word or its concept. So much time. So little time. Tick tock goes the clock.

When my bus arrived we boarded it together. She handed the driver a sealed envelope. I turned and gave her a hug. She went down the steps and walked away. I found a seat in the very back, so that no one was behind me and I could keep an eye out.

At the first stop, somewhere in Kansas, the driver revealed to me the contents of the envelope that he had been handed. It was a note telling the driver that I had been in prison for eighteen years and to look out for me and not let me wander off at stops and forget to re-board the bus. It was signed by the Deputy Warden. The bus driver was very friendly, but the request to him was unnecessary. I kept my eye on that bus. I wasn't going to be left behind.

We arrived in Sioux Falls, South Dakota, early in the morning and were told there would be a six hour layover. Sitting in the lobby I became restless. A beer would sure go over good, I thought. Not pruno, but the real stuff. I left the bus station and walked quickly down the street until I came upon a convenience store about a block away. There I bought two quarts of beer and asked the clerk if she wanted to see my ID. She shook her head and looked at me like I was a weirdo. I was thirty-six years old.

I went to a park and drank the beer. I got drunk. Making my way back to the bus station, I happened upon a cathedral where there was a wedding going on. As I came closer I saw that all the guests were of Asian extraction. Curious, I entered the church and sat down in one of the back pews. I asked the fellow sitting next to me where they were from and he told me they were Vietnamese. After exchanging vows in their language, they proceeded down the aisle and out into the sunlight. I followed them outside and congratulated them. No one seemed to mind that I was the only Anglo there or that I knew neither the couple nor the guests. They just smiled and shook my hand. It was wonderful to witness the celebration of people embarking on a new journey when I myself was celebrating the same. I was moved.

Back at the bus station I called my sister Teresa to tell her of the delay. Her husband, Tom, said he would come and get me. They lived only about an hour away in North Dakota. Tom arrived and we shook hands. He guided me to a white Ford van and we headed to a farm outside a small town (with a population of less than 1,000), where my sister and her family lived.

When we arrived, Teresa met us in the driveway. She still had the same dark reddish brown hair and thoughtful brown eyes that she'd had in childhood and hardly looked her age. We embraced and there were tears in her eyes. She said several "hellos." My heart was full of joy. It was so good to feel welcome and be in the loving cocoon of family. Everything was going to be great. I knew it.

I was wrong. Teresa's husband considered me lazy and saw me as nothing more than an ex-convict with an alcohol problem, among other issues. I saw myself as simply playing catch-up on the eighteen years of fun and living that I had missed out on. At least that's what I told myself. The truth was that I drank in an attempt to consume the fears that were consuming me.

If there were re-entry programs in existence when I was released, I wasn't told about them or given access to their assistance. I was paranoid around crowds and seldom left the house, so finding a job or creating a supportive social network was near impossible. It felt to me like everyone was moving at an incredible speed –an alarming speed –and it was supremely uncomfortable for me. My difficulty transitioning into the free world was frustrating for all of us. I feared that I would not be able to make it –and I knew my sister's help and hospitality would only be available for so long. I desperately wanted to make it. I was breathing free, fresh air, walking down dirt roads without leg irons and watching dragonflies dart and dance. I felt alive. But I also felt afraid. Drinking softened my fears, but doubled my trouble.

My sister had two boys, ages eight and five. In return for staying in their home, I looked after the children while they worked and kept the house clean, doing laundry, etc. It was a wonderful experience being around children. They speak honestly and will talk about how they feel without hesitation. I envy parents for having access to this purity of thought and emotion through their children. After the toxic social-emotional atmosphere of prison, this purity was for me like a blood transfusion.

The kids and I enjoyed each other's company. We didn't do anything special. We built things with Legos, watched TV and just hung out, but we had fun doing whatever it is we were doing. We watched the movie Fantasia together numerous times. One of those times, I asked the boys if they understood why the little boy and his horse sank in the "swamp of sadness" and neither said they did. I told them that it was because he let the sadness overcome him. I told them that no matter what bad things may happen, to never let the sadness overcome them. They responded with solemn nods. I think they understood. What's more, I think they understood that I was speaking from my own experience.

I was awaiting my first disability checks so that I could get a place of my own when my sister came home early saying that my Social Security Disability counselor wanted to talk to me in town. We drove to the highway and found it blocked by Highway Patrol troopers. They pulled me out of the car and put me in chains. They said they were taking me to the State Mental Hospital because of a court order filed by my brother-in-law and approved by the local judge. They told me I was going to be treated for alcoholism.

I felt so betrayed and abandoned. In the Sherriff's car I kept my head down and didn't speak at all.

In the State Mental Hospital I was locked in a cell. The atmosphere was not much different than prison, except that the people around me were slightly crazier than my fellow prison inmates had been. I spent three months in the hospital, went through a Twelve Step program, got counseling, was diagnosed with bipolar disorder and prescribed antidepressants. Even with all this emotional and psychological support, the place simply felt like another prison. The staff appeared as guards to me—some of them kind, some not. I had been free only two months and was back in a cell.

When they released me, my status as disabled had still not been approved and I didn't know what to do with myself. I lived in an apartment that my sister got for me. I felt rudderless and afraid and didn't think I had what it took to make it. I was so afraid of the free world that I wasn't really free at all. I was imprisoned by my fear.

I walked into a liquor store and handed the clerk a note that said, "I have a weapon in my pocket and will use it if you don't give me the money in your register." She pressed a silent alarm. Within minutes the police surrounded the place and arrested me. I had been waiting for them to arrive. I pled guilty and was sentenced to ten years in the North Dakota State Penitentiary. Three months after re-entering prison, I was finally approved for Social Security Disability –a day and a dollar too late.

Kim

I was a little nervous about this chapter of Mickey's life. I wondered if Mickey's view of the circumstances at his sister's house was the full story. By this point in our collaboration, I knew that Mickey was a kind man and that his heart was in the right place. I also knew that he had deep rooted issues, lots of repressed emotions and a chemical abuse problem. Did he black out and do something he didn't remember doing? Was he inappropriate with the boys? Had he been worse off than he thought he was?

As uneasy as I felt about this chapter, I couldn't bring myself to locate his sister. If there was something dark about this part of his life, I didn't really want to know —and after all, I told myself, this book was about Mickey's memory of his life and if this was the way he remembered it, then so be it. I also thought it highly feasible that his sister and brother-in-law had been sufficiently alarmed by Mickey's drinking to have him hospitalized. His history of losing control, as well as his psychiatric history would justify them being more concerned about his consumption of alcohol than they would have otherwise been. Had I been in the same situation, I too would have been very concerned about Mickey's drinking.

In one of my letters, I told Mickey how easy it was to locate people these days and that he would think the Internet was almost magical. He surprised me by asking if I would find his sister and gave me all the information that he could think of to help me with that task. He told me he missed her and that because she hadn't heard from him in almost a decade, she probably thought he was dead. His desire to find his sister alleviated some of my anxiety, because a man who has done something for which he feels guilty – even if submerged under consciousness –is not likely to want to reconnect with the people involved.

It didn't take long to get a call through to Tom, who by this time was Teresa's ex-husband. I left him a phone message and doubted that he would return my call. But he did and while he didn't have anything positive to say about Mickey, the most negative thing he said was, "He didn't do so well when he stayed with us." He asked quite a few questions about how Mickey was doing and asked for the title of the book twice, which made me think he might read it at some point. He gave me Teresa's phone number and told me that I might not reach her for several days because she would be at their son's graduation. It was very kind of him to return my call and I told him so. He gave me a warm goodbye, "You take care."

I got through to Teresa after already having left a message for her, so she knew the reason for my call and said, "I was so glad to hear from you. I have spent the last three weeks praying to God for help finding my brother. You don't know how hard I've looked for him. Since 2005 I've followed every trail that I could think of, but they all came up with a dead end." She wanted Mickey's address and information on how he was doing. Even after all the years without contact, she remembered that it would soon be his birthday and wanted to be sure that she got a card to him on time.

Teresa called me after her son's graduation when she

had sufficient take to talk so that I could ask her questions about Mickey. My first question was what their childhood had been like together. This was her response —and she broke into tears several times while talking:

Mickey was my playmate. He and I did everything together when we were little. He was a good playmate and a cute kid. We were so attached that he was lonesome and sad when I started kindergarten. He was just four at the time. Sometime during my first week of school my mom and I saw him cut an earthworm in half and say "There, now you have a friend."

Mickey was never a child. He was born smart and wise and grown-up. He was all business —He always had "business to do." He was also always getting into trouble and he was too smart so he would find ways to get into trouble that wouldn't occur to other kids.

In his whole life, Mickey didn't ever get a single break. Life has been cruel to him. He was treated terribly wherever he went. The reason we got moved from our first foster home was because our foster mom slapped him across the face so many times that I threatened to run away if we weren't taken to another home. I remember that one of the times he got slapped was because he was using our foster mom's scissors to cut paper. It was never anything more serious than that. They were so mean to him --They were mean to both of us, but especially to him. They locked him in his room constantly.

Our mom was a drug addict and had psychiatric issues, so we never knew what to expect from her day to day.

Twice she came at us with a knife, threatening to kill us. The second time, I was thirteen and Mickey was eleven. She threw us out of the house, threw our coats at us and locked the door. It was winter and we didn't have shoes on. We walked two miles to our grandmother's house.

[I interrupted at this point to note that Mickey's first stint in a correctional school occurred when he was about eleven. I wondered if this nightmarish incident with mom had led him to begin to get in trouble with the law. Teresa thought the two could be connected]

The other time that mom threatened to kill us with a knife was before we were taken to a foster home. Mickey was probably too young to remember. Sometimes I think it's these incidents that caused Mickey to feel so poorly about himself. I felt poorly about myself too –I mean, if your own mom wants to kill you, you must be a really worthless and horrible person. We didn't understand that it was the drugs and her mental instability, so we took it personally.

[I asked Teresa to talk about when Mickey came to stay with her after his release from prison]

When Mickey came to stay with us, he came without medication. He didn't have his haldol, his anti-psychotic medication. I got him a prescription as soon as I could, but he was already unstable enough that he wasn't taking the prescription regularly once he had it. He was fairly stable for a time. He did some painting work for my husband's business and would come home saying, "Tom has me holding a paint can on a ladder in one hundred degree weather. It's killing me." He didn't understand that this wasn't unusual cruelty, but a typical day in the life of a painter. He hadn't ever had experience with kids and so wasn't exactly sure what to do with them. He felt insecure about his ability to take care of them, but he loved to watch them. He was entertained by them and amazed at how smart they were. He loved being called "Uncle Mickey."

But one day he wouldn't come out of the basement. I asked him what was going on. He said, "There are people around that are trying to hurt you." He was delusional about where he was and what year it was. It took me two hours to talk him out of this agitated state. Even after two hours he wouldn't come out of the basement, but I got him to calm down. Later that night I was coughing and he must have heard me because he came halfway up the stairs and shouted "Is he hurting you?! Is he hurting you?! Let me know if he is hurting you!"

I called the state hospital the next day and had him put in. If he would've taken his medication and stayed stable I would've done everything I could to help him, but I'm not equipped to handle him when he's beyond reason and I had the kids to think about too.

After he got out of the state hospital I got him set up in an apartment. We got him a bike and were working on getting him a job. There wasn't counseling or halfway houses or local AA meetings. There was no kind of support for him. He would call me and say "what do I do? I don't know what to do?" Prison ruined any chances that Mickey might have had to make something out of his life. For his entire adult life up until this point, he had been told what to do, where to go and when to do *it. He'd never had to purchase groceries or cook a meal. He'd had his clothing and room and shelter provided for him. He'd never had to pay a bill. He didn't get any kind of training or preparation for living in the real world. He wasn't taught how to think for himself or make decisions or even how to work hard. I felt so sad for him. I don't know how anyone could've expected him to make it.*

If he had been in a position where he could've helped others or contributed in some way it would've done so much for him. He had never had a real job on the outside. He might've had jobs in prison, but that's a whole different world, a slow and easy pace with no responsibilities before or after the job. We were looking for work for him that might be a good fit when he robbed the liquor store and was sentenced to ten years for armed robbery. He didn't have a gun, but they charged him with armed robbery. That's just the way it has always been for Mickey.

Mickey is wise and such a philosopher. He would be a great teacher. He was always such a patient teacher with me. He taught me yoga by drawing pictures of poses and mailing them to me from the penitentiary. He taught me everything I know about religion. I wouldn't get half of what he was trying to teach me and would ask question after question. He'd patiently answer my questions and find new ways of describing something until I understood it.

Mickey wasn't given the skills to excel in the world, but he excels in prison. He's practically lived his whole life there, so that's where he feels confident. I love my brother.

Knopfla Soup and Sweat Lodges

The prison was a two and a half hour drive from my sister's house. I called to ask her if she would visit me. She declined, but said that she'd forgiven me and that she loved me.

I served the full ten-year sentence in the Maximum security prison in North Dakota. It was an easy prison. Inmates got along well, both with each other and with the staff and we were even allowed to call the staff by their first names. Most inmates were content to just kick back and serve their time. What stood out most for me about this prison was its highly German personality. Eighty percent of the inmates were Native American, but the staff and most of the white inmates were ethnic Germans. In mess hall we were served German dishes like Knopfla soup and black bread at every meal. The food was better than any jail or prison fare I had ever sampled. They were lenient with television too. Televisions could be purchased in the canteen and for ten dollars a month we could get twenty-eight channels and HBO. They offered Pell Grants for those who wished to attend college and I signed up, eventually earning an associates degree in Liberal Arts.

My favorite class was World Religions, which was no surprise to anyone who knew me. The class gave me information about various faiths but not direct experience and so I vowed that I would explore some of the faiths and philosophies further when I was released.

After getting an associates degree, I got a job in the

sign shop. My task was to letter street signs. I made one dollar an hour, which is good pay in prison. But I stayed true to my pattern of throwing wrenches into the well-running machinery of my life and used my money to purchase the marijuana that flowed freely there. Three times I was given a random drug test and three times my urine tested positive for marijuana. Each time, I would be sent to The Hole for fifteen days and any good behavior time that I had earned would be taken away. This is why I ended up serving the entire ten year sentence. But I was never fired from my job in the sign shop and for that I was very grateful. I am a better and happier man when I am working and doing something useful with my time.

My best friend, Scott, was a leather worker who worked in the hobby shop where the inmates could work on certain crafts. He could make anything out of leather and would sell it to the staff. He also set up a pruno brewing station in the ventilation system and we would have a "happy hour" about once a week. He was eventually sent to minimum security prison --- "The Farm" -- where he promptly stole a van and escaped. He was caught the next day, on his way to Mexico where he had a wife. He was a short-termer and had no business escaping. I confronted him about this when they returned him to Maximum security and he sheepishly agreed that he was an idiot. But then, I didn't have a wife on the outside waiting for me. I had never had a woman to long for, so who was I to judge?

During my decade there, only one homicide occurred. A man smashed a young fellow's head after he made fun of the man's burned face. Apparently he was very sensitive about his face. He was taken to the Hole and later charged with murder.

Along with my introduction to German cuisine, I was also introduced to the spiritual world of the Native Americans. Because there was such a large population of Native American inmates, the administration allowed them to build a sweat lodge on the yard. I sometimes attended, smoking the pipe to purify my mind and allowing the hot steam to purify my body. It was a deeply spiritual ritual and they took it very seriously, so I did too. A Sioux friend of mine told me a story that went like this: A grandfather spoke to his son and said, "There are two wolves in every man, fighting for his soul. One is good, the other evil." "Which one wins?" asked the boy. "The one you feed," said the grandfather.

The time spent in the North Dakota prison was easy time, a sort of incubation phase for me, a peaceful time after so many years of being moved around and witnessing (as well as causing) so much violence. The dust storm that had constantly been whirling around in my psyche had finally been allowed to settle and for the first time, I felt somewhat consistently at peace. But while my time there was easy time and served a purpose, it was still time in prison and in December of 2000 I happily bid the place farewell and headed to Arkansas, thoroughly convinced that I would never again enter a prison.

All the Wrong Moves

Just two days later, I regained consciousness in an Omaha, Nebraska jail. The last six months of my ten year sentence were spent in a prison in Minnesota. I had volunteered to move there along with about one hundred other inmates. When I was released, two guards drove me to the nearest bus depot and as soon as they left, I took a taxi to a Wal Mart and bought a thermos, stopped at a diner and filled my thermos with coffee, then went to a liquor store, purchased a pint of vodka and after I had sipped about half the coffee out of the thermos, filled the remainder with vodka. The bus drove south during the night and all the while I sipped on the vodka and coffee, soaking up every sight and sensation of the free world. By the time we reached Omaha for a short layover, I was drunk and while waiting at the bus station I experienced a blackout. I wasn't used to that amount of alcohol. When I came to, I was in a cell in the Douglas County Jail. They told me that I had overturned a pinball machine. I didn't remember a thing. Grace had it that the charge was a misdemeanor and entailed only a fifteen day jail sentence, but I had been free only two days and had already landed myself in jail. I felt enormous shame and remorse.

When I was released from jail fifteen days later, I was very relieved to find my bus ticket among my possessions and boarded the very next bus to Ft. Smith, Arkansas, overwhelmingly grateful that I was still a free man. I promised myself that I would never again take another drink. But true to form, I broke that promise almost as quickly as I made it.

I had been invited to stay with my Grandfather, but he kicked me out when he thought I was stealing money from him. My Uncle Gordon thought my Grandfather was misjudging me and being unfair and rented an apartment for me. He was very kind to me and believed in my innocence when I was later arrested again.

I was much more ready for life in the free world this time around, but still had intense periods of fear in which I didn't want to leave my apartment for days or even weeks at a time. My periods of fear were precipitated by anger. I worked temp jobs and while I worked hard, diligently and as efficiently as I could, at some tasks I worked too slowly and was ordered to speed up. Prison is extremely idle and what little there is to do is done slowly. It had been decades since I had moved at the same pace as the world and neither my brain nor my body remembered how to move quickly. There were tasks that fit my pace well and on which I performed well, but I was sometimes inexplicably taken off these tasks and put on tasks that were too fast for me. I, along with the other temp employees, was sometimes treated in a demeaning way by the non-temp employees. Because I was an ex-con, I knew my employment was more precious and precarious than most and so I did not rock the boat or show anger when I felt I was being mistreated. My repressed anger would build until I feared I might lose control and do something I'd regret. I didn't see this pattern at the time, but I see now that I wasn't so much afraid of the world when I'd lock myself in my apartment, but afraid of what I'd do if I went back into it. I didn't want to mess up and so put myself on lockdown. Overall, however, I continued to carry the centered, peaceful feeling with me that I had cultivated during my ten years in North Dakota and had some very enjoyable experiences, even with jobs. I worked for a Christian company installing hot tubs and thoroughly enjoyed the work, the pace and the autonomy.

I also enjoyed my leisure time. Ft. Smith is a town steeped in history and I would often visit a neighborhood in the old district. I would walk down streets with beautifully restored nineteenth century mansions and imagine the parties that had gone inside them: genteel men out smoking cigars and drinking mint julips on the balcony, with the street corner gas lamps illuminating the night. Other times, I would take a good book and sit on the hill next to the restored courthouse of the "hanging Judge" Parker. The gallows was still there. I would sit reading away the afternoon above the Arkansas River, sometimes pausing to watch a barge glide by. It was Spring and I felt leisurely and good.

One day my cousin came up with a win-win scenario. I had an Aunt Nora who lived in Las Vegas. She had recently been diagnosed with Parkinson's and my cousin suggested that she fly me out to live with her in a caretaking capacity.

Although she was my aunt (she was divorced from my dad's brother) she was not my biological relative and there was not a great divide in our ages. There was a strong attraction between us and I fell in love with her. She was easy to love. She was both strong and gentle. She let adversity roll off her like a duck in water. She didn't carry many grudges and could forgive those who did. A landscape artist for many years, she had an artist's eye for beauty. She saw beauty everywhere. She was sensitive to the needs and feelings of others, to the extent that she could put her hand on a person and feel what they were feeling. I never knew her to be inaccurate in her "readings." She had the most disarming smile and it would quickly dissipate my anger or troubled mind whenever I would indulge in negativity. In the company of her gaiety and free spirit, the quantity and quality of my smiles and laughter increased with every passing day.

Affection was something that was alien to me after so many years in prison, but with Nora it came easily and naturally. There was freedom in her touch and to hold her in my arms was what the poets would call, "heavenly." One night she left our house in the middle of the night and when I awoke and saw that she had left I was filled with anxiety. I went looking for her and found her two blocks away at a park. She was sitting on a bench with a bottle of chardonnay, wearing only one of my shirts. I joined her and we opened the wine. After a while we walked further into the deserted park and made love on a grassy knoll with only the sky as our blanket. I was so in love with her that my heart was overflowing with contentment.

Nora was generous with her love and affection. She was very good to me. When I broke my ankle she did for me what I had difficulty doing for myself and my coffee and breakfast would be ready when I awakened each morning. But no amount of love or affection from Nora could quell my fear.

I was afraid of the outside world and felt certain that I would never be accepted into its circles. As Garth Brooks sings, I've only ever had "friends in low places." I was immensely afraid that I would lose Nora. She was accepted by the social elite and traveled in their glamorous circles. She lived so far above me that it may as well have been another planet. I couldn't fathom ever being more than a little moon, a small chunk of rock, orbiting her world and viewing it from a distance. For me, it wasn't a question of whether I would lose Nora, but when. I didn't know what spell she was under that caused her to love me, but knew it would one day be broken and she would see me for who and what I really was. I could not leave her, but the fear of her inevitable departure and the pain that would accompany it was excruciating. I knew the longer she stayed the deeper into love I would go and the greater the hole in my heart would be when she left. So I sped up her departure by demonstrating my most unloveable qualities, the qualities that I felt made me unworthy of her. I was shiftless, irresponsible, unmotivated and while I didn't take drugs or drink hard liquor, I drank beer and far too much of it.

My plan worked and about six months into our relationship Nora gave up on me and went to live with some friends in Los Angeles. I was heartbroken, but relieved that I was no longer waiting for the blade of the guillotine to drop. I ended up homeless. It was humiliating and physically uncomfortable, but there was an emotional comfort in being back at the bottom with my "friends in low places." I was back where I belonged.

Kim

I emailed Mickey's uncle with questions about prison protocol. While I was at it, I asked if he was Mickey's paternal or maternal uncle and this was his response:

I am not related to Mickey at all. He had, in my opinion, very sorry parents, grandparents, aunts and uncles. The reason that I know this is that I was married to one of his aunts. As far as I know, all of his relatives except his sister are dead. Mickey asked for help locating his sister, but I wasn't able to find her. She hadn't attempted to contact him in ten years, so I figured she probably wanted nothing to do with him anyway. I felt sorry for him, the way that his family treated him. One of his last living relatives, a paternal grandfather, lived in a very large house by himself, and when Mickey got out of prison and came to Fort Smith, his grandfather would not let him live in the house. I rented him a small duplex in town and he lived there until he moved to California.

Homeless

One night I set up camp in a desert wash—a mostly sandy place where floodwaters flow during the rare Nevada rains. I had a warm sleeping bag, had built a fire and was cooking ramen. Another homeless man was nearby and asked if I'd like to trade a blanket for some of my food. I readily agreed, not because I needed a blanket, but because it looked like he hadn't eaten in a while. It simply felt good to share, even if it was such meager fare. I've learned that no matter where you go, people are the same. It's just as possible to know joy in a desert wash as in a three million dollar mansion. The only thing the rich or the poor take away with them when they go is the joy they feel for what they have given.

My approval for disability had still not come through, but I'd had enough of Las Vegas and figured that if I was going to be homeless, I might as well find a new place to explore. San Diego called to me and a friend who worked as a night nurse agreed to give me the bus fare. We arranged that I would meet her at the hospital during her night shift and she would give me the money. While walking across a road with a speed limit of 50 mph and multiple lanes, I was hit by a car that didn't have its headlights on. The impact threw me about fifteen feet and my leg was badly broken. I was a scruffy somewhat drunk homeless man. The driver of the car was the wealthy --and probably also drunk-- wife of a powerful casino owner. I was given a ticket for jaywalking and she was sent on her way. Lucky for me we were in front of the hospital. They brought me in, set my leg with a screw and less than twenty-four hours later, my leg throbbing with pain, I boarded a

Greyhound to San Diego armed with a bus ticket, a small satchel of belongings and a system full of Percocet.

In San Diego I decided to honor the vow that I had made to myself while in prison and began to investigate every church, temple and religion that I could find. I attended Catholic mass, Lutheran gatherings, and went to the churches of Baptists, Pentecostals, Jehovah Witnesses, Latter Day Saints, Episcopalians, and Methodists-- which was the church in which I was raised. I later checked out Scientology as well. My experiences with the various religions were an interesting experiment. I met some loving and good people and satisfied my curiosity, but found in none of them the deep Divine connection that I feel when meditating or the reverence and awe I feel when observing the beauty and intelligent design of a flower. I realized that I carry my church with me and that my favorite kind of church service is sitting outside at dawn, admiring and appreciating God's creation of a new day.

I moved a little South to El Centro, where I became a guest for a month in the home of a friend and his wife who were Seventh Day Adventists. I attended temple meetings with them every Saturday and found it to be a thoroughly loving experience. The head minister would sit in on my study group and listen while I compared Satan with the ego and he'd make a comment like, "Oh Mickey, sometimes you are so Eastern!" and we would all laugh. And then he would quietly say, "And we love you anyway." I didn't want to overstay my welcome, so I headed out, directionless and homeless.

In a way, I chose homelessness, because despite its discomforts, it was the freest way of living. There were no bills to pay, no schedules to follow, no standards to live up to, nothing at which to fail, no one telling me what to do or how quickly to do it and nothing tying me down when an urge for change came upon me. At this point in my life, for obvious reasons, I valued freedom more than just about anything else and was willing to endure the disdaining looks and discomfort of homelessness. I was also homeless in part because I spent too much of my disability check on alcohol and weed. I was hurting over the loss of Nora and craved emotional escape more than usual. When I was hungry and my disability had run out, I would do odd jobs for restaurants—window washing, cleaning sidewalks, bussing outdoor tables-- in exchange for a meal. There were moments when I was happy and I was free and getting by.

One cool night I was sleeping on a sidewalk in San Diego with about ten other homeless people, bundled in blankets obtained from the Salvation Army. I was awakened by a man mumbling to himself. He was tall, well over six feet, with wild, wiry red hair down to his shoulders and an overgrown beard to match. I watched as he paced up and down, bending over occasionally to pick up imaginary insects and "eat" them. He looked like he was in withdrawal from opiates or alcohol. "Bro," I said quietly, so as not to awaken my sleeping companions, "are you alright?" He only mumbled so I said louder, "Come here for a minute. I can help you." This he seemed to have heard and he came tentatively to where I lay propped up on an elbow. I shook out two klonopin tablets (my anti-seizure medication) and gave them to him, along with a half-pint bottle of whiskey with which to wash them down. He took them and then handed the bottle back with shaking hands. "Now sit here a while and you'll start feeling better," I said. He obeyed. Within an hour he quieted down and I knew he would be okay, at least for a while.

After a time he spoke with clarity. He introduced himself as Tim and thanked me for the help. He looked at me with sky blue eyes that I could tell didn't miss much and gave me the address to his apartment in Tijuana. He said to visit whenever I wanted and I said I would. He then walked away on steady legs and I rolled over and fell asleep.

About two weeks later I decided to pay Tim a visit. I'd had a job for a time in a restaurant kitchen and when payday came, I figured it was a good time to travel to Tijuana. I arrived at Tim's apartment and passed through a gate that was open and found myself in a compound with half-naked children playing. Tim's apartment was up a flight of wooden stairs and his landlord lived below him.

When he answered the door, a look of surprise crossed his face, but he recognized me instantly and said, "Mickey!" with welcome in his voice, "Come on in man!" He smiled as I entered and I was glad that I had come. After that day I'd cross the border into Tijuana occasionally to visit him.

Tim was crazy, but his craziness was something I liked

about him. He was also a heroin addict and a Vietnam vet, one having to do with the other, as his first fix happened there. He was a few years older than me, in his late forties, but when he talked about the war in Vietnam, he became an impassioned youth of eighteen, still ducking and dodging bullets. He spoke with awe about a "Tree-Shooter," an American sniper who sat camouflaged in a tree for hours at a time, knocking off the enemy whenever one of them would enter the jungle. "He never missed," Tim would whisper while cooking a shot of heroin, "not once."

During my visits with Tim we would get high. The Tamale Man would stop by and deliver tamales and drugs. I smoked some of the best marijuana of my life there —and the tamales were delicious-- but I never went to anything harder than that. Tim would shoot heroin and I would smoke the weed while sitting in an overstuffed chair across from him. He would speak in a slow drawl, occasionally nodding his head. When his chin would nod to the point that it was resting on his chest, I would announce that I'd be taking my leave and return in a few days. He would be just barely alert enough to shake my hand and I'd walk out and flag a taxi to the border. I'd walk through customs with the bag of marijuana in my pants while they x-rayed my pack. I was never caught, but my heart would pound so hard that I feared the customs agents would hear it.

Tim's landlord didn't allow overnight visitors in Tim's apartment and so when I decided I'd like to stay in Tijuana for a while, I booked myself into a long-term stay budget hotel. It was not what most would consider luxury accommodations, but to me it was paradise; a place of my own, my own shower and toilet, no roommate, a big window and a door that I could open or close anytime I pleased. I was the one in charge of the lock and key.

I found the nature of Mexico to be beautiful, with its desert mountains, streams that trickle into the ocean and the variety of cacti. Tijuana is not a beautiful city, but the sky above it is and each night and most mornings it would treat me to hues of pink and orange. The people are also beautiful. Most are willing to share their food and even their lodgings with a complete stranger. Many have very little money and use food as currency. I once rode a one-peso station wagon cab stuffed full of people. Next to me sat an elderly man with a rooster in his lap. The chicken would peck my shoulder from time to time while the old man sat stoically staring forward. I assumed he was on his way to trade the chicken for something. I was happy to get to where I was going, because that bird had a mean beak!

One night I stopped in a park, sat on a bench and sipped on liquor that I had in my pack. Two Mexican cops on bikes grabbed my pack and began searching until they found the marijuana. They arranged that they wouldn't throw me in jail for having marijuana as long as I gave them all my money. I took all the money out of my pocket, placed it on the ground in front of them and one of the officers said, "American border two miles north. Do not turn around." I knew I was very lucky not to have ended up, not only in prison again, but in a Mexican prison and I did not look back until I had cleared customs and gone into San Ysidro. I was never able to visit Tim again. Thankfully I had become pretty street savvy by then and had twenty dollars still left in my shoe to hold me over until the next round of Divine intervention.

I hitchhiked to Yuma, Arizona where I met another kind couple at a Seventh Day Adventist Meeting. Their names were Fred and Wilma and they offered me lodging in their fifth wheel trailer in exchange for caring for their cactus garden, trimming their desert palms and irrigating their orange grove twice a day. They were elderly and needed the help and I enjoyed working with the plants and being outdoors in the desert. The old couple spoke very little, except when I would accompany them to meetings each Sabbath. Wilma was withdrawn and didn't trust me and so rarely said a word to me. Fred was kinder and more outgoing, yet he too spoke little to me —perhaps because Wilma didn't want him to. This didn't distress me; I had a place to live and a small way to earn my keep and for this I was very grateful. In contrast to Fred and Wilma, their beagle fully enjoyed my company and would accompany me on my rounds and then sit with me in the trailer.

Their property was cut out of the desert and right on its edges were desert scrub and barrel cacti. I loved the Arizona desert. I would find a place to meditate each morning before dawn, when the shadows were still long and the sun more gentle. The energy there was ephemeral, dry and crisp. I would sit with eyes closed and focus on my breathing for close to an hour. It was a daily ritual that recharged my spiritual and emotional battery. On one occasion I felt something looking at me and opened my eyes to see a Gila Monster sitting about two feet away, watching me intently. He blinked rapidly at me every few moments and then had his fill of looking at me and slinked away. I liked watching the hummingbirds too, such beautiful little birds and so fast. After a few peaceful and happy months with the old couple and the cast of desert creatures, I called Nora's daughter and gave her the number for the phone in my trailer. I quickly received a call from Nora, who by that time had returned to Las Vegas and missed me, which is testimony to how forgiving her heart was. I had felt her absence like an amputated limb and could not wait to be with her again.

For years I had dreamed of living in a cabin in the mountains. I have always felt best in the mountains. I had told Nora about that dream while living with her previously and she had liked the idea too. She was calling to say that she had located a cabin for rent in the San Jacinto Mountains that rise seven thousand feet above Palm Springs. With our combined incomes (we were both drawing disability checks) we could afford to live there. Without further ado, my benefactors wished me a safe journey, said a prayer and I bid them a fond and grateful goodbye as I boarded a Greyhound bus. My anticipation grew as the bus got closer. To not only live in the mountains, but live there with Nora by my side was beyond what I had ever hoped to experience. I was really excited and excitement is a feeling that has been rare in my life.

Kim

The letters that Mickey has written have taught me as much about Mickey as the stories that he has written for the book. The unexpected length of time it took to complete the book gave us the opportunity to test the waters with each other, feel more secure and gradually let down our guards and unfurl our deeper personalities.

For the first few months, many of Mickey's letters contained mostly philosophical or spiritual discourses. I wasn't sure if he was sharing his beliefs with me with the goal of helping me to get to know him better, thinking out loud as a way to pass the time, or sharing his wisdom in the hope that I would glean inspiration or illumination from his words. His motivation may have been all the above. As time went on and his letters became less philosophical, I realized that these letters had been his safe zone. My safe zone had been to focus on book tasks, with a smattering of very superficial details about my life –the kind of details business colleagues might share during a game of golf. Keeping the relationship a business relationship provided me with a safe vantage point from which to observe Mickey and test him out before crossing the line into friendship. As instantly connected as I felt to Mickey, I was wary. I had been fooled before, both by others and by what I thought was my gut instinct.

Mickey and I were both playing it safe, but there was a major difference in where we stood on the chessboard of our relationship. While I was strongly called to work on his book with him and everything about the project felt right, if he showed himself to be someone with whom I didn't want to have dealings, I knew that I could easily opt out and move onto something else that would fulfill me. For me, staying in the game was much more risky than not staying in. For Mickey, the stakes were high. I was not only the midwife that would help him deliver his book to the world, but I increased his social connections in the outside world from two to three. I was one third of his outside social network and the only one who showed promise of becoming a close friend. My goal was to test Mickey and see if he passed the test. Mickey's goal was to pass the test.

Mickey's spiritual and philosophical wisdom is perhaps the only aspect of himself in which he feels some level of confidence. He is extremely well read and well versed in these subjects and has successfully used his wisdom to support, comfort and console others. In other words, this is what Mickey believes to be his best side and so this was the side he showed to me in the beginning:

Dear Kim,

…I have come to believe that the light is in us now and that enlightenment is merely recognition of this fact and not any kind of change at all. Sometimes I think we get lost in the seeking and by looking elsewhere for the light, we miss experiencing that we are it, right here and right now. And right here, right now is all there really is. We are eternal. There is no past, no future, only an endless now, a seeming extension of time that we call "the present." Onto the present, we project the past and the future; one behind, one in front, but they don't really exist. The present, this holy instant, is the only truth. Focus here and now and you will find peace and surcease from pain…

Over the course of our collaboration, I continued to ask Mickey for more details, more candidness and more feeling in his stories. I wanted to know more about his shadow side, the side that had gotten him into so much trouble, so many times. He was very slow in providing these details. At best, they trickled in, one, maybe two at a time. At the time, I thought this was because he was accustomed to harboring, not sharing feelings and that digging up his past was painful for him. This may have been so, but later it occurred to me that the primary reason for his reticence was that he didn't want to scare me away.

I have always believed that if people really got to know me, if they got close enough to see my shadow side, they would no longer like me —or at least not like me as much. As my friend Carter theorized, Mickey and I are much the same person, the difference being simply a matter of scale. I think Mickey felt fairly certain that if I were to know all there was to know about him, I'd make a hasty exit from his life. He didn't want to lose me as editor or friend and so mum was the word. I was waiting to see what he was really made of, because while he was incredibly likeable on the surface, I needed to see what was underneath that likeability before I'd decide whether or not to take this into a real friendship —and to give my own full disclosure. We were stuck, both in our literary venture as well as our friendship, because both would only be really good with full disclosure.

Our friendship's —and the book's —salvation came in the form of disaster, as it often does. When I read

Mickey's letters to Bo and Sita and freaked out, Mickey's fears about me were realized. He sensed that I was making my exit, or at the very least, had decided to keep my distance and not become the friend that I had shown the potential to be. He was so hurt that he finally got angry and showed me a little of his shadow side. His shadow side, it turned out, wasn't scary at all –at least not to me. His dark streak had damaged him plenty over the course of his life, but to me his anger was nothing more than defensiveness and a couple of very minor digs at my character. His anger, it turned out, expressed itself like a hurt little boy, which is precisely the place that it was coming from. Ironically, by getting angry at me, Mickey proved to me that he was safe and I began to let down my guard. After several more apologetic letters back and forth with each other, I began to commit and he began to disclose.

Mickey's stories began covering more of the times in his life when he had screwed up, times that he felt ashamed of himself. He saw that I still thought well of him, even though he had made such a mess of his life. What's more, he began getting feedback from me regarding others who had read his stories who felt moved by him and thought he seemed like a goodhearted man. People were getting to know about his every lackluster effort, bad decision, crazy episode, selfishly motivated action and screw-up and seemed to like him anyway. Probably for the first time in his life, Mickey had a group of people outside of prison –a group who knew the good bad and ugly about him – who thought well of him.

The tone and depth of our letters began to change. We became more chatty, talking about the everyday minutiae that friends talk about.

"I have this insidious electrical outlet that sometimes throws out a flame, scaring the shit out of me. I just plugged in the hotpot to heat water for tea and it did that. I had to push the reset button, timidly. Drat! I wish it did not do that."

For about a month we forgot that "it" wasn't about finishing a book, but about enjoying the journey of writing, storytelling and deepening our friendship. We got irritable with each other and got nothing accomplished, but even this was progress, because it showed that we felt secure enough with each other to be less than pleasant. We supported each other, not only in getting back on track, but staying there.

At my request, Mickey filed the necessary paperwork so that I had access to his status and records —and so that I would be notified in case of an emergency. He didn't think the prison would allow me access to his information if I wasn't a relative, so he listed me as his aunt. I began signing my letters "Aunty Kim." I made half a dozen calls to the prison's medical offices in order to get him a doctor's appointment when the prison suddenly stopped issuing him his anti-seizure medication. When I got very sick twice in the span of three weeks, Mickey took on the uncle role and kindly but firmly told me to slow down and rest.

"You've been driving yourself too hard and you are fatigued. You need to slow down. There is plenty of time to get done what needs to be done. We need you in good health. Okay? Okay!"

Our friendship began spreading farther and farther outside the realm of book collaboration.

I began to share when I was overwhelmed –which is often. Mickey has shared his brief moments of self-pity--- but always rallies after a paragraph. We've supported each other through some losses and commiserated about schedule delays. Mickey's deep peacefulness slows down the perpetual motion machine that seems to live in me. More than his words, it's the calm energy behind his words that causes me to slow down and hear the birds singing or my children laughing or really sink into a hug from my husband. I feel myself taking deep slow breaths when I read his letters.

In turn, I am the fire igniter for him. I re-light his pilot light when his motivation flags and he sinks into the habitual lethargy that comes from a lifetime of failures (why try anymore?) as well as the idleness of prison. I remind him that he has something to offer and that it's something wonderful. When he gives less to his stories or his life less than I know he's capable of giving, I tell him so and ask him to raise the bar on himself. I am both a cheerleader and a well meaning but highly annoying coach. I have high expectations of him and am willing to be a mosquito in his ear if necessary to get him to be what I know he is capable of being. He finds me highly irritating, but he also loves me.

"Take away time and there is only now. Take away space and there is only here –and somewhere between here and now is where I love you, dear friend! ☺*"*

Dream Come True?

Our cabin had two bedrooms and was situated directly below a mountain peak. We were surrounded by ponderosa pine and Manzanita and our back deck rose twenty feet above a meadow. A family of coyotes lived in the meadow and I would occasionally throw them bones. It was idyllic. A dream come true. I was not going to make the same mistake with Nora that I had made in Las Vegas and so this time I gave her everything I was and did everything I could to live up to the second chance that she was giving me.

She and I hiked up a mountain trail nearly every day and we'd see deer and even eagles. The beauty of that place filled so many empty spaces and recharged my spirit. Because she was weak from Parkinson's, Nora had difficulty with the hike, so I would walk in front of her. She'd hold the back of my shirt and I'd pull her up the mountain. It was such a small thing, but it meant so much to me to be useful to her, to support her in some way and show that I was there for her. I used my disability check more wisely and this time we were a financial team, paying the rent and bills together. I supplemented my income with local landscaping jobs and enjoyed the work. I even managed to buy a car. Nora and I spent most of our time together and thoroughly enjoyed each other's company. I believed I would live out the rest of my days in that cabin, hopefully with Nora by my side.

Nora and I contacted my sister and told her that we were a couple and living together in a cabin above Palm Springs. Teresa was thrilled for us and began putting together plans to visit. It was wonderful to have my sister in my life again. I was also blessed with the company of children. Nora had young grandkids and when they would visit, the little neighbor children would come over and I'd don a scabbard and crown from the toy chest and let them chase and beat me. When I would pretend to die, they would say "No stay alive! Stay alive!" because it was only fun if I was alive and chase-able. They would wear me out and it was the very best kind of tired.

Nora and I had the dream of collaborating on greeting cards. She would provide the art and I would provide the poems and sentiments. We had a boutique in town willing to sell them when we had our line ready. I felt complete. I had more than I had ever dreamed as being possible for me.

The dream turned nightmare six months later. Nora was a complex person with a lot of psychic wounds and it's obvious that I was the same. She had a beautiful heart, but it was her external beauty that she believed had been her ticket to play in the rich and glamorous circles of the "beautiful people." It was her external beauty that she felt others valued.

Her Parkinson's disease and medication had caused her to gain weight and had accelerated the aging process and her tremors were worsening. As she lost her beauty she panicked and looked to me for validation that she was still attractive. I knew that she was really looking for validation that she was still valued and loveable and did my best to show her that she was. While I saw my love for her as real, I could not believe that her attraction toward me was anything more than a physical, sexual attraction. She lived out the fantasy of being in love with the "bad boy," because I was an ex-con. I accepted this, because being with Nora under any conditions was far better than being without her.

And it got even more complicated. On the one hand, she would encourage me to drink because drinking unleashed the "bad boy" aspect of my personality, as well as the fact that I tended to treat her as more sexually desirable when drunk. On the other hand, she had been in an abusive relationship and had been beaten when alcohol was involved, so my drinking made her nervous. She was afraid of my drinking and my history of losing control when I drank. She never asked me to stop drinking, but there was a constant push-and-pull from her where drinking was concerned.

This is the only photo I have of Nora. She was upset at the time this was taken because our neighbor was spanking a child.

It was New Year's Day and while Nora was in town, I drank shots of tequila left over from the New Year's Eve festivities. I had asked her to pick up my acid reflux prescription while she was in town, but she didn't get it for me. She had also hidden the food. She felt me losing control as I drank too much and was getting very nervous. She wanted me to stop drinking and knew I had such severe acid-reflux that I could not tolerate alcohol without the medication and food in my stomach. But I didn't stop drinking. I didn't even slow down.

When she came home without my medication, I was enraged. In the beauty and quiet safety of that mountain I had finally come to the realization that I was no longer imprisoned, that I could now make my own rules and live life the way I wanted to live it. Nora was motivated by concern for me and for her safety, but I couldn't see that. I could only see someone manipulating me, trying to control what I did and did not do. Something in me burst and all those years of being confined, treated unfairly and manipulated came rushing forth in one strong current. I didn't see Nora, I saw every prison guard and every judgment and constraint ever imposed upon me.

According to her, she went to bed and I came in and punched her in the stomach and told her that I wanted her to feel the same pain that I was feeling because she had refused to get me my medication. She later said that I didn't punch her, but that I had put pressure on her stomach. I don't remember doing this, but I was very drunk and very angry, so it is likely that this is true. I later came back again and confronted her with a knife in my hand. I didn't do anything but make threats, but threats from a man with a knife in his hand who had once killed someone with a knife must have been terrifying. I really scared her.

She called 911 and told them that I had once killed a man and that she was afraid I would kill her. She left the cabin after making the call and went next door to stay with the neighbors. When the deputies arrived, they asked me if I had tried to kill her. I told them that was so much nonsense. We had simply argued.

They arrested me for "brandishing a weapon," but later upgraded the charge to "Assault with a Deadly Weapon," when they discovered that I was a Three-Striker.

At my jury trial, my aunt testified on my behalf and said she had been exaggerating the incident. She claimed that I was innocent. But the DA played the 911 tape to the jury and they could hear her hysteria and fear. The jury found me guilty in less than two hours and I was sentenced to fifteen years for my prior convictions, plus twenty five years to life under the three strikes law, bringing it to a grand total of forty years to life.

I was stunned. How could this have happened? In the state of California men received lesser sentences for murder. Not only had I not committed murder, I had harmed no one. But in retrospect I saw that I had harmed someone. I made this woman—a woman that was the sun rising in my dark sky and my whole heart--fear for her life and severed the bond we had. Spirit had allowed me to experience the wonders of love and the other side of life. I chose to drink and in doing so, risked losing this gift. How could I have done this? How could I have ruined the first truly happy time of my life and landed myself back in prison, possibly for the rest of my life?

Nora's previous experiences with domestic disputes had occurred in Oklahoma, where the routine was that the police threw the man in jail for the night and she'd get a restraining order if needed. When she called 911 that night, she assumed this would again be the case. She had no idea that I would end up in prison, and certainly not for life. This extreme sentence must have weighed very heavily on her.

I received one letter from Nora after my sentencing, saying she believed I had never really loved her. I think she needed to convince herself that I had not really loved her so that she could also believe that her absence would not leave me heartbroken. The night I got the letter, I dreamed that she came to me with my leather hat in her hands and placed it on my bunk. She then turned, got into a car and drove away. I awoke crying. In my heart I begged her not to go. It was then that I knew I had lost her. I wrote her letters, but they came back to me unopened. It hurt like hell at first, but she needed to move on with her life and couldn't do that holding on to me. Our time was past —a time to every purpose under heaven. But I miss her and probably always will.

Cabinhome

branches of twisting
crooked strands
of old witches
gone to earth
Nights like sweeping
silver trails of light
singing timeless
hymns of nature I
hear the child
of timeless wonder
in remembered dreams
of cabinhome

Mickey Owens

A Cry for Love

A life sentence. I was despondent. Suicidal. The Holy Spirit eventually lifted me out of my suicidal mind and reminded me that wherever I go, He goes with me. I was reminded that there was still a purpose for me and that this purpose was served wherever I went. Maybe I could better serve my God and my fellow man behind bars. In any case, this seemed to be the plan. I let go of my guilt and my fear of the future and with a trust in something bigger than me, headed to my new home; a maximum security prison in California.

After being there for three months I received my classification as Level Four custody, the highest level of custody there is. I was transferred to Salinas State Prison, near Monterey, California. I was there a short time when I was assigned a celly who was psychotic. He often talked about killing his entire family when he got out of prison —something I tried to discourage him from doing.

One night he cut himself with a razor while I was asleep. He passed a note through the door to where the guard would find it while making his rounds. He wrote that I had cut him and was trying to kill him. I was awakened by the cell block's alarm sounding. A few minutes later the door slid open and they hustled him out. They ordered me to prone on the floor and handcuffed me behind my back. A lieutenant asked me what I had cut my cellmate with. I told her that I had not cut anyone with anything. I was totally confused.

They escorted me to a holding cell where a sergeant interrogated me. I maintained my innocence but it did no good. Because I had a record of a crime involving a knife and had murdered an inmate before, I was written up for "Battery with a Weapon on an Inmate" and taken to the Hole. I spent six months there before I was given a hearing and found innocent. But that would not give me back the six months I spent in that stinking hole. I came away from there angry and resentful and it was a long while before the Holy Spirit took my pain and replaced it with forgiveness.

A few weeks later I was transferred to Kern Valley State Prison, a newly built level-four prison. I was one of the first inmates to live there. The yard was still dirt and there were no chin-up or parallel bars nor tables. It would take months for those things to arrive. In the meantime we were kept in our cells for weeks on end.

I had a cellmate from Los Angeles who was quiet and nice. He was there on parole violation and got out after a few months. He was a heroin addict and I encouraged him to check into a methadone maintenance clinic when he was released. The celly who replaced him had just come off Death Row after spending twenty one years there. His sentence had been commuted to "Life without Parole." He was the same age as I and we got along well most of the time, which was a good thing, since we spent so much time on lockdown in the same small cell together.

After several months the bars and tables were installed in the yard and there was one for each race. I worked out on the bar for the Whites and one day while working out, a white dude and his celly began stabbing a man who had just arrived from another prison. The tower guard fired a block gun (a gun that shoots plastic squares and is capable of killing a person if it strikes them in the head) and knocked one of the assailants to the ground. The other was so determined to kill this man that he stayed astride his victim and continued to stab him in the chest. Blood was everywhere. Another guard managed to hit the assailant with a bullet and he fell to the ground unconscious.

We were prone out, belly down, when the ambulance came to take both men away on gurneys. The assailant who had been shot with the bullet died in intensive care. The man who was stabbed miraculously survived. Afterward, all Whites were put on a three-month lockdown.

I don't know why the attack occurred, only that in prison all points are made via violence. They have no idea of the karmic reactions that are set into motion each time they are violent with another, nor of how they hurt themselves when they hurt another.

Not long after that incident, I grabbed a guard's arm, upset that he wasn't paying attention to a mistreatment going on right next to him. Guards are jumpy in high security prisons and he reflexively pepper sprayed me. In response, my reflex was to get angry and knock the pepper spray out of his hand. A group of officers extracted me from my cell and worked me over. I was sentenced with "battery on a peace officer," and sentenced to eighteen months in a prison that held even tougher criminals than the one I was in.

I was put on a bus to the Corcoran SHU, in Corcoran, CA where I would serve an eighteen month sentence for the "assault" on the guard. When the lieutenant discovered that I was there for assault on a peace officer, he ordered the guards to treat me roughly. They maintained a hostile attitude toward me and I was scared of what they would do to me. I tried to explain to them that I hadn't assaulted the officer, but had just grabbed his arm to get his attention, but they didn't believe me.

After completing my eighteen month sentence, I was transferred to Delano, another hostile prison. My new prison was the home of Charles Manson. By then he was just a crazy old man in a wheelchair who would one day die there. He was very generous with the other inmates though and one time shared his instant coffee with me. Kindness is kindness and in prison, one takes kindness wherever it is found.

I had never before experienced anything like the "politics" of California prisons. The toughest of the tough are in these groups, the kind who view prison as a step up in their group's hierarchy. Prison is part of their gangster career ladder. There are three groups of Mexicans: The Serranos, from Southern California, the Nortenos, from Northern California and the Pisas, from Mexico. My celly was a Pisa from Tijuana. The Serranos and Nortenos hate each other and fight and stab at every opportunity. The Nortenos run with the blacks, while the Sorrenos run with the Whites. Within the Blacks are the Crips and the Bloods, while the whites are broken into far more diverse groups: Aryan Brotherhood, Skinheads, Nazi Low Riders, Sac Rats, etc. Each of the groups forbids contact with the other groups, which creates an atmosphere of division, ignorance and hatred. Most of them bond together for safety, but the "us versus them" feeling that comes out of this type of grouping and separatism ends up leading to more violence. In the end, everyone there is more at risk, even those who are not involved in the groups.

I was there about two weeks when a major riot occurred in the dining room that was situated in the center of our quad. It wasn't a riot against the staff, but inmate against inmate, Blacks versus Southern Mexicans. A Mexican had celled-up with a black and the Southsiders would not tolerate it. There were about one hundred inmates fighting in that dining room. Only the whites stood to the side and were left alone. Eventually the guards intervened with pepper spray and we were locked back in our cells.

In the thirty years that I had been doing time, I had never felt pulled to join a group or to in any way separate or differentiate myself from others. As I matured I felt more unity with my fellow man than separation and refused to adhere to the limited thinking and divisiveness of these groups. This has gotten me into trouble at times.

The Skin Heads ordered me to stay away from other races and when I refused, they snuck up on me from behind, grabbed my head and yanked it backward into a headlock. The one holding my head had his arm over my eyes so I couldn't see what was happening or how many were there. They cut my throat and cheek with razor blades and stabbed my chest. I believe I would've been killed that day except that the knife they used to stab me in the chest was dull and something went amiss. I heard one of the Skin Heads say, "The chain broke" and this seemed to unravel their attack. A guard fired a block gun at them and everyone immediately dispersed. I was taken to the hospital where I received twenty- eight sutures.

This experience changed me. The attack was completely unexpected and was the closest I had ever come to death. An inexplicable peacefulness came over me. For the first time in thirty years, I felt some peace over having killed a man. I do not know the cause of this peacefulness. Maybe the attack was a way for me to work through the karma caused by my having killed a man. Maybe it was simply that in facing death, I provided an opening for Grace to come through. Whatever the case may be, I am grateful, both for my life and for the peace that is still with me today.

My assailants were charged with attempted murder. I don't know what became of them. I never saw them again. But I have forgiven them. In their actions I heard, not a cry for murder, but for love. Love isn't part of their beliefs or their world view and they walk around with gaping emotional holes because of it, holes they protect with every variety of defense and weaponry. I guess I've been enough like them to understand.

Kim

A man who was formerly a designated hit man for the White Supremacists in an Oklahoma prison sent me this story while Mickey and I were collaborating on the book. His story is a beautiful illustration of the "cry for love" that Mickey says he saw in his assailants.

Two Sacks of Cookies and One Whole Heart

I have been a drug addict for most of my life. I was first introduced to weed and methamphetamines at the age of nine and I stayed high from nine until the age of twenty-five. As a result of my drug addiction, I have been in prison twice since I was eighteen.

But the purpose of my writing has more to do with the time when I was dating a woman who was pregnant with my child. I love her and I worked hard to support her. I dropped out of school partly to work and partly because school didn't appeal to me. I was working two jobs, one as a plumber's helper full-time as well as at a restaurant in the evenings.

My girlfriend and I got engaged and everything was fine until the day I walked in on her having sex with her father. I freaked out and tried to kill myself. I wound up in a mental institution and as they say, I "faked it until I made it" and upon my release hit the ground running with drugs as my prime focus in life. I had regressed to the point that my family pled with the courts to incarcerate me so that I would be forced to receive some type of treatment. I ended up in trouble with the law and was sent to prison for the first time as an adult in August of 2003.

I carried my anger around me like a blanket. I was always fighting and getting into trouble. I was always harassing and hurting people who had committed sex crimes. I had discovered that the woman I had been engaged to had been raped as a child and that this is where her issues stemmed from. I had a daughter by this time and she lived in the same household with her emotionally messed-up mother.

At one point during my incarceration, I signed up for a Kairos weekend. I was really only wanting to go because I knew they would bring snacks every day. But God had a plan and a purpose for me beyond getting snacks. This program was about Christ and God and at that point in my life I believed that Jesus was who he said he was, but I was far from having any kind of relationship with Him. I was still drugging and selling dope in prison. I was what's referred to as a "prospector" for the White Supremacy Gang and this role required me to do what this group told me to do. They would order me to stab someone or fight a guy and take his TV and I would do it. It was with this kind of violence that I filled my days.

I would also seek out those who had committed sex offenses and extort them and cause them all kinds of turmoil. I was sick, twisted and demoralized and controlled by my next fix or high. My hatred toward sex offenders burned deep. I was scared to death that my daughter was going to be molested, so I felt justified doing whatever I did to a sex offender.

But then God stepped into the scene at the Kairos weekend. From the start, the staff at the retreat talked to us as people who were worthy of love. I don't know about any of the others, but I didn't feel like a person who was worthy of love. These people had the most amazing love I had ever seen. It was a love that can only come from God.

We talked about such things as forgiveness, love, redemption and God. Every night there were people sharing about their lives and

I found myself in their stories. I would say things to myself like, "Man have I been there" or "That's me in a nutshell." Then they started to talk about how God in His love had forgiven them and how their families had been restored and how God in His infinite love continued to bless them. This is when I could no longer relate to the subject. I knew nothing of God's continuous blessings.

There was an altar call at the end of each night and they would invite us up to the front, assuring us that there was nothing to be afraid of and that if we came up, they would pray for us and with us. I decided to go. I wanted to go, but felt very nervous. I probably looked like a deer caught in headlights as I stood up. But at the same time I felt a gentle presence tugging on my heart and thoughts and comforting me. I asked someone if they would go up with me and was surprised when they agreed. We went up together and I asked God to come into my life and to forgive me.

Instantly I felt a wholeness that is hard to describe, like a piece of me had been missing and had finally been put into place.

At the end of the first night they gave us a sack of cookies to take back with us to our cells. At the end of the second night, they talked about forgiveness; how God has forgiven us and how, likewise, we should forgive others, even those who have harmed us. They then handed out the cookies, but this time handed out two sacks of cookies and told us that as an act of forgiveness, we should find someone whom we have a problem forgiving and give them the second sack.

I went back to my housing unit and the guards called count, so I stayed in my cell during the count, thinking "Great, I have TWO sacks of cookies!" But then guilt caught up with me and I thought that maybe I should do what they had asked us to do. I thought about people I've had a hard time forgiving and couldn't come up with anyone, so I decided to ask God what He wanted me to do, believing that I wouldn't get an answer and that my sweet tooth could then get the two sacks of cookies it wanted. I was startled when I heard a voice clearly say "What about my children whom you have failed to love?" Like a movie, I saw that dreadful night in which I found my fiancé with her father. I saw my daughter's pictures and felt my fears for her. I thought of all the harmful thoughts and actions I had directed at sex offenders. I knew what God wanted me to do and I had never been so scared in my life. I sat down, crying out to God, "I can't believe you want me to do this. I can't do it. I won't do it."

I tried to tune out God by picking up the newspaper. I found an article about Jeffrey Dalmer the serial murderer. It was about an interview given by a reverend saying how Jeffrey had given his life to God and how the inmates were always giving him a hard time. He said the people who gave Dalmer a hard time were people claiming to be Christians. Jeffrey asked the reverend, "What part of the blood of Christ can save them, but can't save me?" These Christians were persecuting another Christian, another of God's children, same as I was. I said, "Okay God, I got the message."

I spent the rest of the inmate count in my cell praying for God to give me the strength to do what I needed to do. When we were cleared to leave our cells, I grabbed the cookies and walked by a guy's cell a few times, nervous and scared. I finally knocked on his cell and went in. I can only guess what he was thinking when he saw that it was me. He probably thought he was about to get beaten and lose his TV. I sat down on the stool at the table across from him and asked him if he was a sex offender. After a little stammering, he said that he was. At this point, it is probably hard to guess which of us was more scared.

I closed my eyes for a moment and cried out "HELP" with every fiber of my being. The same gentleness that I had experienced at the Kairos retreat settled over me. I began talking to this guy about what had happened to me the previous two days. I told him my fears about my daughter and how I have held on to my anger in order to justify my actions. Then I talked about what had transpired in my cell during count. I told him about what I had done to people who were incarcerated for sex crimes. With tear-stained cheeks, I asked if he would forgive me for all that I had done and I handed him the sack of cookies.

As soon as I asked his forgiveness, I felt the blanket of anger thrown off me. He said that he forgave me and even thanked me. I asked him if he was saved and he said he wasn't, but if God could do something like this with me, he was willing to ask God into his heart.

We held hands and prayed together.

It is now years later and I am back in prison on a probation violation, but still hold love and compassion in my heart and treat people kindly. By the grace of God I am sober and doing well. I have a peace that surpasses understanding.

Written by Cody Rogers

Pleasant Valley

Shortly after I was attacked, I was transferred to my current home, Pleasant Valley State Prison, where I have been for a little over three years. The energy here is oppressive and dead. The only people who are not afraid to smile and freely laugh are the guards, usually at some poor sod's misfortune. There are some here who are able to forgive their tormentors and it's those men to whom I gravitate and welcome as friends. This place has been a test of my spiritual fortitude. It is a ghetto of social and emotional sickness. Minds are twisted here and suicide isn't uncommon.

I have chosen a celibate lifestyle. I miss affection, especially after having given and received affection in such abundance with Nora. But affection doesn't exist here. We all want it however. Some attempt to find some semblance of it through gay relationships, as I did in Oklahoma, but those types of relationships are mostly about the release of pent-up sexual need, not affection. Those who have the means to do so make appointments with the barber, simply so that they can be touched.

Others substitute affection with drugs and alcohol. Some repress it, like so many other emotions that are repressed here, and they become hard inside. I do my best to surrender to a Higher Power to meet my needs. I am not always effective in this, but it is the best way that I have found to cope.

There is no affection, but there is love. Some join up with their home-boys and become a friend 'til the end, sworn to watch each other's backs when danger comes 'round. That is love.

Love is also expressed by some inmates who attend Christian ceremonies, and in a more etheric and spiritual sense by those who see beyond the veil and understand that love is all there is and that the more love is expressed, the more love comes in return. Love creates more love and asks only of itself.

There is also compassion. Recently a friend of mine caught a man stealing from him, which violates the convict code of ethics. He caught the perpetrator in the act, walked in on him in the cell and asked "What are you doing in my cell?" The fellow answered, "You have so much and I have nothing," at which my friend softened and said, "Okay, take something and leave and do not come back." The fellow thanked him profusely. I was proud of my friend.

There is also love in my memory. I sometimes sit on my bunk and reminisce about my time with Nora and experience a rush of joy. Her smile still lives in me. And who can say, maybe one day I'll see that sacred place in my heart again with someone new. Who can say?

My Uncle Gordon has been my only family connection to the outside world for eight years. He lives in Arkansas, so is not able to visit, but he orders a care package for me every quarter and has done so for many years. Uncle Gordon was also the one who so generously took my original handwritten stories for this book and typed them for me. He is seventy-nine years old and has cardiopulmonary disease. He requires constant use of an oxygen tank, so his efforts on my behalf are even more appreciated. I am very grateful to him for his support and his belief in me all these years. He is such a good man, a God-send, and I don't know what I would have done without him.

I have been on the waiting list for a job since I arrived here. There are a thousand men and very few jobs, so it may be a long time before I have something to occupy my time besides books and my twelve-inch television. During a normal day, I awake at 5:30 am, make coffee quietly so that I don't wake my cellmate, meditate for an hour and then go to breakfast. My cellmate is Mexican and speaks very little English, but we are nice to each other and our good intentions toward each other are more bonding than any words. We are friends, which is good, because we are often in our small cell together twenty-four hours a day on lockdown.

If we're not on lockdown we are allowed into the day room each day and into the yard a few times a week for anywhere between one and five hours. The grass in the yard is green during the Spring, but brown during other seasons. There was once a baseball diamond, but someone used the metal that anchors the bases to create a weapon so it is no longer used. Four times around the yard is approximately a mile and I walk it until I am tired so that I will sleep well that night. There are almost one thousand men in the yard at the same time and no trees, awnings or overhangs to shield us from the blazing summer sun or the chilly rains. When violence erupts or the guards see a threat of violence, each of us sits down wherever we are until the situation is resolved.

The term "day room" conjures up a sunny, comfortable image, but it's just another cement room, with some kind of plastic over the windows. In the day room we can move around a little and there are some metal tables and chairs on which the men can play dominoes and cards.

Fights break out all the time and pepper spray is regularly put to use. There is an elevated control tower in the middle of the room and when necessary, the guard will shoot a block gun (non-lethal, but hurts like hell) or if there is a stabbing or an attack on the guards he will use the rifle and may kill a man. There are signs on the walls that say, "No Warning Shots." Nothing much is new in these places. One day is like a thousand others, even fights and stabbings. We come to expect the sensational as much as the mundane.

Many men band together as gangs in an effort to secure their safety, but then get lost in the violence instead. They can't be stopped with words, but I can live my life as an example and hope that they will see that only through kindness is safety established. Kindness begets kindness. What goes around comes around. People don't usually want to harm someone who is kind to them.

No one tries to recruit me into their politics anymore. I am too old and the story has circulated that I was stabbed because I wasn't willing to participate in any groups. I am left alone for the most part and in a place filled with so much anger and aggression, I prefer being on the sidelines.

In the dayroom I interact a little with others and when

requested, I transcribe letters for those who can't write or help them prepare court appeals. I would like to share what I know about spirituality. I would like to talk with others about what has given me peace and a feeling of value, but the guards often get nervous when the groups are too large or we talk for too long. If they're feeling nervous, they are allowed to break us up if we talk for more than five minutes. In any case, most of the men here are not open to believing in something different or more, so these kinds of conversations don't happen frequently.

I have always been an introvert and I don't interact much, but I am not alienated. I quietly offer help when needed and in that way, I fill my need for both connection and being useful.

Overall, my days are fairly idle, with little conversations and television filling the time. I write letters or poems and meditate. It was here that I began writing this book, with the hope that people might get something positive out of my life experiences.

When I completed the original manuscript, I had no idea what to do with it and no knowledge about book publishing. Just a week after completing my manuscript, Kim appeared out of "nowhere" and began pouring her energy into its transformation. She was right on time, as if we had both planned it that way. But we have had some tough times. We have been irritated with each other, grown impatient with each other and at our lowest, distrusted each other. Kim can be relentless and at times I have been exasperated with her. I think she would say much the same about me, except that it's my stubbornness and occasional inertia that exasperates her. But we've got a bond that has weathered all of this and I believe it is a bond that goes back before this lifetime. I believe we have been close in other lifetimes. She is my mentor and my very dear friend.

Dear Kim,

...Most inmates in the California Penal system will tell you that kindness in prison is a joke, a myth and if you think you witness a guard being kind, it is only because he is afraid and is pacifying a man long enough to read how much of a threat the inmate poses to his safety —in other words, it's a defense technique and not true kindness. After spending eight years in California prisons, I've come to agree with this assessment in most cases, yet there are exceptions and I recently experienced one of them.

The reason you haven't heard from me in a few weeks is that I have been in the hospital —I got your letters after I was returned to the prison and am really sorry you were so worried. I knew you would be and I felt terrible, but I just had no way to reach you.

What happened was that I found out that I had pneumonia and in the middle of the night I was told that I was being transported to a hospital. I was so weak that I could hardly walk and was shivering with chills. I also had sharp pains in my lower abdomen. I was put in an orange short-sleeved jump suit (no jackets allowed) and a guard walked me across the yard in the cold rain to a waiting van. I was shivering and shaking while they chained me up and placed me in the vehicle. In the van was a male and female officer to guard me.

In the emergency room, they placed an IV in me which required several sticks because I have bad veins. The entire time, the guards sat expressionless, vigilantly keeping an eye on me.

They wheeled me to an MRI and discovered that I had an

obstructed bowel and would need emergency surgery. Back in the emergency room I was pumped full of pain relievers. From another room, I could hear a child sobbing, the sound of children is something I never hear in prison and the sound of a child crying tore through my heart. I looked straight into the eyes of my female guard. I could see pain and concern in her eyes and for a moment, I didn't see a guard sitting there, I saw a mother, her maternal instinct bringing a tear to her eye. I was so moved that I asked the nurse what was wrong with the child. The nurse said the child was not a patient, but visiting a family member who was. The guard and I looked at one another and sighed with relief.

An hour later, two others showed up to relieve the guards. Before leaving, the female guard walked over, squeezed my shoulder and said she hoped I would be okay. And then she smiled at me.

So yes, I do believe kindness can be found in prison and an expression of it, no matter how small, is a treasure and a reminder that within all of us is a heart...

Love,
Mickey

Light Up This Joint

Over and over Kim has asked me to put more into this last chapter. She says it lacks the soul of most of my other chapters. After many months of trying to give her what she's asked for, it occurred to me that the problem is that I haven't had the soul to give to this part of my story. My spiritual journey has had its ups and downs, its ebbs and flows. Sometimes it's been easy for me to feel the Spirit and sometimes God has felt so far away as to be almost nonexistent. I have found myself in one of those times.

Sometimes it is hard to feel grateful. Sometimes it is hard to see the Light. Sometimes it is hard to find meaning to my existence or to feel Divine support in the living of it. But being aware that this has been an ebb in my spiritual tide and that I am in control of the flow, helps me. The word "repent" in the Bible was originally a Greek word meaning "to face another direction." I know the Light is always in my life and that seeing it is dependent upon me looking in another direction –to take my focus off the many shadows and dark spots in this place and look back toward the Light.

I am now in the Autumn of my life and as much as I wish for it, I will not likely take my last breath in a mountain cabin, but right here, in a house of steely architecture and steely dispositions. My cabin in the mountain was heavenly, but I know heaven is accessible anywhere, even in Pleasant Valley State Prison. It's simply a matter of facing another direction. Sometimes a simple turn of the head, even a slight change in focal point, takes monumental effort, but I am making the shift and once again beginning to feel at peace. I believe that God is a happy God and is even happier when we are happy. I look at a card that Kim sent me, on it are butterflies rising up and she has written "Rise up and the whole Universe rises up with you." That is my intention.

Kim says she believes there are people on this planet whose *soul* purpose it is to anchor the light for the rest of humanity, to keep the Divine flame burning through the dark nights of the collective Soul. She thinks I am one of these people. I can feel the truth of this. I may live in a 6'x10' cement cage, but in me lives darting dragonflies, the pure play of children, peaceful afternoons along the Arkansas river, a mountain meadow, a family of coyotes, the kindness of strangers, the hugs of friendship, desert sunsets, Nora's smile, the never-ending love of my mother, and the wings of the Holy Spirit. They carry me high above the steel and concrete in which my body resides, to a place where there is only light, life, joy and love. I soak up the goodness until I am ablaze with it, carry it back with me to my cell and really light up this joint.

Epilogue

As we were putting the final touches on this book, I received an unusually brief letter from Mickey. My heart lurched into my throat when I read "This is the last letter I will be writing," but resumed its normal position when the sentence ended with "from this prison." He was being relocated to a prison in San Diego because of its medical facility. He neglected to tell me why he needed a medical facility. I assumed this omission was due to the fact that it was something too serious to bring up in a hastily written letter and so was certain that he was dying for the two days it took to get his next letter. In that letter he told me that he has Hep C and a broken screw in his leg, but that he was primarily being moved because of his epilepsy —all old ailments and aches, which I assume have become higher maintenance due to age. I'm grateful for their higher maintenance status, because they gave Life an excuse to create some movement and change for Mickey.

It had never occurred to me (nor do I think it occurred to Mickey either) that he would or could ever move. I think both of us figured he'd be in the same prison until his last breath. I was excited for him. Granted, moving from one maximum security facility to another isn't anything to get too excited about, but I had a really good feeling about it. He had been in a state of positive expectation for a while and I just new this move was a positive outpouring from that positive state of mind.

In his follow-up letter, Mickey said:

I have been at Donovan since yesterday. There were no cells open so I spent the night sleeping on the floor of a large holding cell. They told me I would have to forego my bottom tier/bottom bunk order if I wanted to move into a cell today, so I did and am sleeping on the top bunk.

[Epilepsy and a top bunk didn't seem to me to be a safe combination]

My cellmate is Cambodian and does not understand English, but can speak a few words. He is seventy-nine years old —a reminder that a life sentence is really a life sentence. We communicate with gestures and hand signals. He seems a kind soul.

What is strange is that my celly at Pleasant Valley was from Mexico and only spoke a few words of English. The Holy Spirit determined that since I cannot travel to experience diversity, He is bringing the diversity to me in the form of my cellmates.

Speaking of Mexico, it is right in my backyard. I can see houses in Tijuana nestled among smoky hills. On the ride down from Pleasant Valley, we passed through Los Angeles and in Marina Del Rey the ocean came into view. We had sight of it all the way past San Diego. I hadn't realized how much I missed it. There are seagulls and pigeons sharing their space with us. The seagulls float on the air currents with the backdrop of the Mexican hills. It's a majestic scene and worth bringing out your brushes and paints for...

We are on lockdown after a massive search of the prison, but I'm hopeful it will end quickly. I am experiencing what they call "relocation fatigue," which can take a few weeks to get over. It's an illness we get from acclimating to so many years of the mundane and sameness. Change is a jolt to our systems..."

He told me that the San Diego prison was rumored to be a nicer prison and an easier place to "do time." He made note of the fact that it is located twelve miles from the ocean. I told him I hoped those good ocean ions were able to reach him twelve miles away.

Despite the lockdown and his relocation fatigue, he sounded a little rejuvenated, a little lighter and brighter. I continued to feel positive about his move.

One of the reasons I felt so positively was that this move opened up the possibility of seeing him in person. His previous "home" was out of the way enough that neither my frequent flyer miles nor my schedule made it easily accessible. I assumed it would be years, if ever, that I saw Mickey. But San Diego I could get to. I go there regularly to visit a couple of my dearest friends. I have intended to live there since I was seventeen and am certain I will get there one day. It might be that Mickey and I will live in the same city not too long from now. The way things have gone with Mickey and me, this seems likely. I wanted to see Mickey in person and have a real live conversation. So ten minutes after hearing about Mickey's move, I switched a trip I had planned to Florida and booked a flight to San Diego instead.

Within an hour, I had researched the hoops I needed to jump through in order to visit Mickey. Turns out prisons don't make visiting easy. I needed Mickey to sign and then mail me a visitor's application. I would fill out the application and mail it to the visitor's department where they would do a background check on me that could take up to thirty days. When my visitor's pass was approved, the prison would notify Mickey who would then mail me a letter letting me know of my approval.

When I visit, I must not wear clothing with any metal, including an underwire bra. I am not allowed to bring him anything. I am not allowed to carry a purse, only a small clear plastic bag. I cannot have a camera, phone or even more than two keys on my key ring. But I was surprised to learn that this would be a "contact visit." I would not have to talk with him through glass. I could give him a hug when I first arrived, could buy us lunch and have a photo taken with him.

I couldn't wait for him to find out I'd be visiting. He hadn't had a visitor in eight years and I doubt he expected that I would ever visit. It was like throwing the best surprise party ever. I counted the minutes until the mailman came each day and eagerly opened the mailbox.

But his letters stopped coming. I had yet another eye-opening experience about the life of the incarcerated and the people who care about them. Mickey writes almost every day, so I grew more apprehensive with each day that passed without a letter. Suddenly his "Relocation Fatigue" seemed like it could have been something more. Did he have a seizure that gave him a heart attack? Was he in a hospital all alone? I am not normally the type to jump to these types of conclusions, to fear the worst, to be such a worrier. I normally teeter on the edge of Pollyanna, but my experiences surrounding caring about someone who is incarcerated have changed me. My complete lack of control over communication with Mickey, with what got through to him and what didn't and how long it took to get to him had rendered me helpless. All the stories Mickey had written about the horrible things that happen to inmates and the way many of them suffer and die alone had taught me to expect the worst.

I called a dozen numbers at the prison –almost every category given to me by the prison's phone directory – and either received a recording that directed me to another number or a recording that asked me to leave a message. I left messages at three of the numbers explaining my concerns and asking if I could be told whether Mickey was okay or not. I did not get a response –not even to tell me that I wasn't allowed access to that information. I put out a prayer request to my facebook network. At least thirty people said they'd keep both Mickey and me in their prayers and then many continued to check in and ask if I had heard anything. Mickey had a lot of love directed his way.

It occurred to me that Mickey's uncle was probably listed as next of kin and so would likely know if anything had happened. I emailed his uncle and he told me that when an inmate is relocated, they are not allowed to bring anything at all with them –not even a piece of paper or a stamp –and so the lack of communication from Mickey was most likely due to the fact that he didn't have anything to write with. I immediately put money in Mickey's commissary account via the prison's pay-pal like system, but figured that because Mickey had run out of money, it was unlikely that he would go to the commissary and discover that there was more money for him. And anyway, he might be in the hospital. All alone. I felt totally helpless.

That same day, I finally received a letter from him. Based on the fact that he didn't yet know that I would be visiting, nor that he had several additions to make to the book, I knew he had not received my *eight* most recent letters. Not only had he not been able to write me, he hadn't been getting my mail either:

> *"...We are still on lockdown and I am now hearing that it may be a month or so before we are up again. I haven't yet received my property from Pleasant Valley, so don't have television to keep me and my celly occupied. In two of my previous moves my television never made it to me and I was forced to buy a new one. I've collected a number of magazines and books for something to do. I just finished reading; Harry Potter and the Deathly Hallows and loved it. Harry destroys Lord Valdermort at the end. The 700 pages helped pass the time.*
>
> *I have been here six days and still have not been issued clothing. I've been wearing the same blues that I was given upon my arrival. I wash my underwear each night with state issue soap in our steel sink. It's pretty primitive here right now. I traded deodorant for six stamped envelopes, which is how I was able to write you this letter...*

Mickey then went on to apologize, yet again, for our rough patch a month prior:

> *"Kim, I am sorry if I have in any way offended you or hurt your feelings when I wrote those negative letters to you.*

I thought you were trying to belittle me and that you lost trust in me because of my letters to Bo and Sita..."

My lack of correspondence had led Mickey to think that I might be distancing myself again. He was getting worried. I needed Mickey to receive my letters so that he would not worry. I needed him to know that I was visiting so that he could send me a visitor's application and it could be processed before I visited. With less than a month until my trip to San Diego, I was worried for the both of us.

I made another round of phone calls and this time got a live person in the visiting department. I told her of my predicament: I would soon be flying from Oklahoma to visit Mickey, but he wasn't receiving my mail and so didn't know to send me a visitor's application. She said she couldn't help me. She said if she notified one inmate, she'd have to do the same for all inmates. I told her, as politely as I could, that this was not actually the case, that she could just tell one inmate and not all the others, but she held firm. She was close to ending our call when I said, "Look, I have never been to a prison before and don't know the ropes. I am helping this inmate write his memoir." At this point she warmed up a little and I assumed it was because I wasn't just a "regular" family member or loved one, but someone who had business with an inmate. I assumed that if I had been someone who "merely" deeply cared about and missed an inmate, I wouldn't have gotten the same assistance. She agreed to transfer me to the counseling department for Mickey's cell block, saying his counselor might notify him for me, but not to get my hopes up. I thanked her for her help as she got ready to transfer me and she paused –she probably never hears "thank you" and was wondering if I was serious and also whether she'd really been helpful –before she tentatively said, "you're welcome."

I left a message with the counseling department and asked for a call back to tell me if they were able to notify him. They did not return my call.

A few days later I got another letter from Mickey. He said that he had been told that I had put money into his account. I could feel his relief, not about having money (turns out he wasn't allowed to use it for another two weeks), but that I hadn't abandoned him. He wasn't getting my letters, but he had some reassurance that I was still there for him.

By this point I was feeling upset to the point of outrage. I worried. I stewed. I hated feeling out of control.

I finally wore myself out fretting and spinning my wheels and surrendered, took some long, slow, deep breaths and reminded myself that all was well. An hour later I received a letter from Mickey with the visitor's application.

> "...My counselor called me into her office today to tell me that you wanted to visit me! Yeah! That's the best news I've gotten in a very long time. I can't wait to see you face to face! ☺..."

His counselor had come through for us after all.

Four days later I received his response to a letter that I had sent almost a month prior. He was beginning to get my mail. He was off lockdown. He told me again how excited he was that I was visiting and that he had begun looking into what we could do and how we could order lunch and how long we could visit.

His next letter said,

"Kim, I am able to talk by phone for fifteen minutes at a time on certain days. I haven't said anything about it before because I didn't want to burden you with the cost of collect calls."

What?!! I didn't know whether to focus on the sweetness of his concern over my finances or wring his neck for waiting seven months to tell me this. We could have been talking by phone all this time! Think of the speed by which we would've finished this book! Think about the misunderstandings and delayed drama we would have avoided! And I wouldn't have had the stress about the visitor application and whether or not he was okay. But then I realized that I also wouldn't have had the full story, the full journey and wouldn't have learned nearly as much about myself, Mickey or what it's like to care about someone in prison. Each time I have ranted to Jeff about the latest glitch or wall or speed bump that Mickey and I have encountered, he has smiled and said, "It's another chapter in your book." So true. And isn't that the case with all of life?

Another part of that letter provided a beautiful glimpse, both into his new home as well as his heart:

...I have moved to another cell and this will be my permanent address. I moved in with a friend of mine from Pleasant Valley

who has cancer. I am his caregiver. My friend Man, the Cambodian I was living with, begged me not to move and I tell you, it broke my heart and I wanted to cry. Partings are not easy when someone counts on you to help them. My gut is roiling with pain and my emotions are in conflict. I hope I made the right choice. I love that old man....

It turned out that getting to a phone was much trickier for Mickey than I had anticipated. Besides the constant lockdowns they go through in which they aren't allowed out of their cells, there are also constraints on which days and which times they may make calls. When they are finally allowed to make calls, the competition to get to a phone is fierce —and sometimes aggressive. Once a call goes through the timer starts and exactly fifteen minutes later it abruptly ends.

But one day Mickey got to a phone. He surprised me by having a pretty strong Texarkana accent —think Ross Perot, only (thankfully) a little lower —and a lovely quiet laugh that came easily from him. I could feel his smile on the other side of the line and pictured how incongruent that smile must look where he was. He spoke slowly and calmly, which is the pace and cadence I had expected from him. My instant reaction to his voice was to feel calm. As soon as he said, "Hey Kim," (making my name into almost two syllables, "Ki-em," with an upswing at the end) I went straight to center. Having been married to a man for almost twenty years whose voice has the same effect on me, I know that it's not what they say, but their Zen dispositions that have the calming effect. I thought I would be nervous talking to Mickey for the first time, but I was completely at ease. If he was nervous I could not tell. I told him that I'd had test reads done on the book and that people —even some of my most stoic colleagues — had cried. He was bowled over and had awe in his voice when he said, "Kim, I am going to be walking on air all day, knowing that our book moves people like that."

Phone calls from Mickey provided a way for him to act more immediately on his intuition or sixth sense and the serendipity in our connection went to a whole other level. The most striking moment was the day I found out that my father had died. My brother called to deliver the news: Our father had been taking photos of the "Mega Moon" as it rose over the Hawaiian beach. He had been on his roof deck and although they didn't know how the accident had happened, he had fallen and died. As soon as I hung up the phone, it rang again. It was Mickey, calling on a day that he did not have phone privileges. I don't know how it was that he was able to get to a phone, but if he had called even thirty seconds later, I would have already holed up in my grief and would not have answered. But I was still in shock —and Jeff was saying "Kim, pick up the phone and talk to Mickey" —so I took the call. As soon as the collect call went through, he said, "Kim, how are you?" He spent the allotted fifteen minutes letting me cry and saying kind words in his slow, soothing voice. After our call he wrote me a long letter full of empathy and comfort. Like so many of us, I've struggled to find the right words to say when someone is suffering a loss. Mickey knew what to say. He found just the right words.

On a subsequent phone call, Mickey spoke

uncharacteristically fast, saying that he could only talk for a minute because the men were fighting over the phones. I knew that "fighting" in prison didn't just mean loud or unkind words and I could hear menacing voices near him. I later found out that while he quickly but very calmly spoke to me, he had been surrounded by several men from a Mexican gang telling him that they were going to hurt him if he didn't immediately get off the phone. When I told Paul about this he said, "Mickey isn't afraid and he will not fight. People don't tend to mess with him because they can feel this about him. He believes in peace and is willing to die to maintain this principle."

Mickey may not have been too concerned about whether he died or not, but I was and so I let him talk and talk fast. He said he needed to hear a kind voice because he had just found out that his appeal had been overturned and that now he had no hope that he would ever be released from prison. He believed he would die there. I told him that I was here for him, that he was loved and cared about-- and then he had to hang up because the guys surrounding him were beginning to take action, but even so he took a second to say, "God bless you Kim."

After this call I wrote him a letter and hoped the mail would get to him quickly for a change:

Good Morning Mickey,
On the way to school today, the kids and I took a moment to imagine giving you a good morning hug. It was 6:05am your time, so you were probably just finishing meditating or pouring your coffee.

I heard a quote recently that I loved: "We are entering a time in which we no longer learn through the school of hard knocks, through dark nights of the soul, but through simply following joy." I feel that happening, but at the same time, we slightly "older school" folks are still going through hard times —through rings of fire —that burn off what has been weighing us down and lighten and brighten us up for the brighter journey ahead. I feel that happening for you. One of my gurus, Rev. Michael Beckwith, has a great question for people who are going through extra-tough times. The question is this: "If you knew that your current situation was going to continue indefinitely, what quality would you need to mine out and cultivate in order to make it so that life felt good for you?" That question helps us identify what it is our current situation is calling us to do —or more precisely, what Life is calling us to BE.

Mickey, we all have beautiful souls —because we are just part of one beautiful soul —but your soul is more revealed, more open and available than most. You are a stone and your life has been a raging river that has tossed and banged you over and over again until the rough edges are gone. You are finely polished and beautiful and you are this way for a reason —for a purpose. Mother Teresa was called to the slums of Calcutta to work with the lepers. Ghandi was called to stand and shine love between millions of people wanting to kill the other. You are in maximum security prison, a place where people have forgotten about love, felt abandoned by love —or have never learned that they are loved in the first place, where fear rules the day. What a perfect place for your pure heart to shine and do its healing work. I look forward to being one of your minions and helping you with your mission in any way that I can —and I look forward to learning from you more each day.
—I love you,
Kim

...Turns the Clock...

At 17
A prison scene;
At 21
Nobody's son—
Parents were gone, lives were done
At 29
Still doing time,
But at 36, out of the mix
--only a minute and then back in it—
Northern lights defining scenes,
Sleepy Dakota, icy dreams
At 45
Came alive;
Left that world far behind
California mountain called to me
But freedom there
Was not to be
At 49
Life is my time;
At 52
In the SHU*
At 56
Still in the mix,
But what the hell
Can I say?
Just turn around
And pass the day...
---Mickey Owens PVSP
(*secure housing unit)

A portion of the proceeds from this book go
to:

Miracle Distribution Center
www.miraclecenter.org
3947 E. La Palma Avenue
Anaheim, California 92807
Phone: 714-632-9005

And

Human Kindness Foundation
http://**www.humankindness.org**/contact.html
PO Box 61619
Durham, NC 27715
Email humankindness@humankindness.org

For media and other business inquiries, or to
write Mickey contact:
Kim Whiting
whitingk@cox.net
(702) 524-3231

Mickey and Kim are at work on another book!
To be notified when the new book comes out "like"
our Life Sentence, Life Purpose facebook page or
email whitingk@cox.net

Made in the USA
Charleston, SC
09 June 2012